CU01507416

I was born on 17th April 1923 a   . .. .v...
my parents were working-class, which meant that there was
always a shortage of money. My father had joined the local
agricultural merchants as an Office Boy at the age of 13. He
was very conscious of his lack of education and took every
opportunity to remedy this so that he was eventually able to
teach shorthand, and in the 1940s became Office Manager.
My mother was one of a generation of married women who
never worked and my father agreed with this. However,
during World War II all women were conscripted by the
government to work, and she was directed to a local factory
which made false teeth for the forces! I think she enjoyed the
freedom of mixing with other people and the feeling of
having some financial independence from my father – but at
the end of the war she returned to being a housewife.

In 1933 I went to Ludlow Grammar School, where we had
excellent teachers of Geography and History and, mainly
because of them I became very interested in these subjects –
an interest which is as strong as ever today. My school days
coincided with the rise of Hitler's Nazi Party in Germany, and
Mussolini in Italy. The main objective of both these governments was territorial expansion at the expense of their
neighbours and the peace of Europe was under constant
threat.

In 1938/39 Germany annexed Austria and Czechoslovakia and made the acquisition of part of Poland as the next objective. Great Britain and France became alarmed and finally opposed Germany by guaranteeing Polish independence. This led to the start of World War II on September 3rd 1939.

When the war started I was sixteen and a half and although I was too young to be involved at the beginning, I eventually experienced the Blitz Air Raids in Birmingham followed by four and a half years service as a Navigator in the RAF.

From time to time over the years I have told my wife Eileen about my war experiences and she urged me to put them on paper so that the family and particularly our grandchildren will have a memento to carry to the 21st century. In compiling these memoirs I have been given considerable help by Eileen and my daughter Jane, to whom I am very grateful.

CHAPTER 1

The Storm Clouds Gather

The Second World War began long before the actual outbreak of hostilities in 1939. There have been many books written about its causes, which are very complex. However, the main reason was Germany's defeat in the First World War in 1918.

The German armed forces always claimed that defeat was not on the battlefield but in the collapse of the Home Front due to the Anglo-French sea blockade. which caused starvation.

There is also no doubt that the harsh terms for reparations etc. imposed on Germany by the Treaty of Versailles in 1919 led to bitter resentment and a determination to overthrow it. The poor economic conditions in Europe (with rampant inflation in Germany in 1923) also had significant effect.

However, all these events were beyond my comprehension in the 1920s, and my own first recollection of problems ahead came in 1935 when a public meeting had been arranged in Ludlow Town Hall to explain the work of the League of Nations. The League of Nations was first set up after the First World War and was one of the positive things to come from the Treaty of Versailles. The main purpose of the League was to settle disputes between countries amicably thus avoiding the horrors of further wars. It also had many other functions (e.g. looking after refugees; medical help; education etc). In fact, I remember entering a school essay competition on the work of the League and winning five shillings (25p) first prize! It was very sad that the League failed because of lack of support particularly by the USA (who did not join but had a policy of isolation from Europe) and by Germany, Italy and Japan who withdrew in the 1930s as they became involved in attacking other countries.

Such was the interest in Ludlow about the League and its possibility of avoiding war that the meeting was absolutely packed. My Father took me along to it (admission 6d each). I remember that there was plenty of awareness at the meeting of the danger to peace posed by the attitude of Germany and Italy. A feeling persisted that only the British and French Governments could stop their aggression and they had plenty of grounds to interfere because Germany had broken specific terms of the Treaty of Versailles (by re-occupying the Rhineland in 1936).

When you talk to most people about the history they learned at school, most of them will complain that it was all about dates and battles and was terribly boring! While our history teacher inevitably talked about dates and battles, he set aside one hour each week devoted to current affairs. This involved a study of the First World War reading the excellent volumes compiled by the *Times* newspaper which illustrated the horrors of trench warfare. This had a very profound effect on me during World War II. We also read articles in the *Times* and *News Chronicle* national papers and discussed the political situation and likely course of events in the future. I remember how we came to the conclusion that only a firm

OVER HELL & HIGH WATER

FIRST EDITION
published in 2001
by
WOODFIELD PUBLISHING
Woodfield House, Babsham Lane, Bognor Regis
West Sussex PO21 5EL, England.

ISBN 1-873203-70-5

Over Hell
& High
Water

LESLIE PARSONS

Woodfield Publishing
BOGNOR REGIS · WEST SUSSEX · ENGLAND

Contents

Author's Introduction 7

I   The Storm Clouds Gather 9

II   In the Beginning – 1939 15

III   My First Job 23

IV   Trainee Navigator 33

V   Joining a Bomber Crew 55

VI   Bomber Command 67

VII   A Posting Overseas 115

VIII   A Liberator Over Burma 131

IX   Paradise Island 157

X   The End of my Flying Career 183

stand by Britain and France would stop the German/Italian aggression but Hitler, in particular, was extremely shrewd by claiming to be a bulwark against communism (as practised in Russia), thus protecting the capitalist (free enterprise) system in the West. He therefore had many influential supporters in the UK, France and USA.

When Italy invaded the backward African country of Abyssinia in 1935, it was pure aggression without any justification. Cinema newsreels showed pictures of fully loaded Italian troop ships sailing through the Suez Canal to Africa. The canal at the time was controlled by the British Government. When we discussed this in class we were appalled at British inactivity. This was only slightly changed by the resignation of Foreign Secretary Anthony Eden in protest. This had little or no effect, since by this time Foreign Affairs were conducted by Prime Minister Neville Chamberlain, who actually believed he could negotiate with Hitler and Mussolini. It was like trying to come to an agreement with gangsters.

By 1936 war seemed more and more likely. My father, who felt very strongly about political matters, decided he would join the Army Reserve and had the necessary medical and interview. However, he was not allowed to join, as his was classed as a 'reserved occupation' which frustrated him.

The British government (which was Conservative) had been re-elected with a large majority in 1935 so there was no hope of a change. Ludlow always did (and still does) return a Conservative member of Parliament, but nevertheless, on the day of the election my father's bosses came round to the staff and warned them that failure to support the Conservatives would lead to individual sackings! Of course this was an idle threat, as they had no means of finding out how people had voted, but nevertheless they created an atmosphere of fear due to the high unemployment at the time.

In 1936 I contracted diphtheria, a serious disease which in those days was frequently fatal. A new serum had just been produced to fight the disease and thanks to that, good nursing by my mother and an excellent doctor, I survived – but I was in bed for five weeks and it was six months before I fully recovered.

1936 was the year when Spanish rebels began the Spanish Civil War. The rebels were led by General Franco who was supported by Hitler and Mussolini. German and Italian intervention enabled Franco to win in 1939 and provided battlefield training for the German/Italian forces particularly the Air Forces who began indiscriminate bombing of Spanish towns (e.g. Guernica in 1937) when hundreds of civilians were killed.

To relieve the boredom of being bedridden my father used to buy me several quality papers like the *Times* and I would avidly read about the Spanish Civil War and its effect on the peace of Europe. It so happened that my doctor was an ex-army medical man and he was also very interested in politics. When he came to visit me we discussed the war in Spain and he would ask my views on its progress and likely result.

"The government will win" I used to say.

"I think Franco will win with his backing by Germany and Italy," was his reply.

In the event he was right and I was wrong.

Although I was very interested in Current Affairs in the mid-1930s, I was even more interested in Cricket, Rugby and Association Football. My close friend Syd Lewis and I used to spend hours playing and talking about these games. We still do over 60 years later!

The impression I most remember at this time was that Europe was like an enormous bubble about to burst. We heard on the radio Hitler speaking to enormous gatherings of Nazi followers at rallies in Nuremberg, which were preceded by awe-inspiring torchlight processions. There was no doubt that Hitler was a most impressive speaker and one could sense the tension built up by his words.

The world had already seen Hitler occupy Austria in Spring 1938, important parts of Czechoslovakia in the Autumn of 1938 (through the 'Munich agreement') and the remainder of Czechoslovakia in the Spring of 1939. It was absolutely clear that his word could not be trusted and, sure enough in mid-1939 he claimed part of Poland (the Danzig area) as German territory. Although Hitler continued to deny that he had any territorial ambitions for Germany once his dispute with Poland had been settled, the British and French governments decided to negotiate a defensive military alliance with Russia so that Russia would join in assisting with Polish defence in case of German aggression.

I remember playing cricket in August 1939 and arriving home to see my father looking very agitated waiting at the gate.

"You'll never guess what's happened", he said. My mind immediately thought of some sporting disaster. "Hitler and Stalin have signed a non-aggression pact, which means that if Germany invades Poland, Russia will not intervene."

Now war really did look inevitable and, sure enough, in September 1939 Germany invaded Poland, which was shortly divided between Germany and Russia and although Britain and France declared war on the 3rd September, the immediate effect was negligible. Hitler had conquered Poland and was ready to make 'peace' with Britain and France.

CHAPTER II

In the Beginning – 1939

There are dates in one's life which are never forgotten. In my particular case I shall never forget the events of the 1st, 2nd and 3rd of September 1939. Although it is over sixty years ago, my recollection is so clear that it seems like only yesterday.

The 1st of September was a Friday and we were approaching the end of our school summer holidays. I was up as usual at 6.45am to listen to the seven o'clock news bulletin. (I was an avid news follower in those days, as I am today!) I heard the dramatic announcement that German Forces had invaded Poland in response to alleged Polish attacks on Germany. This of course proved to be false and was an excuse for German aggression. Throughout the morning I listened to every news bulletin. These were very depressing as Polish cavalry and bi-planes stood no chance against German tanks and modern aircraft.

Every Friday afternoon during the school holidays about twelve of us went for a swim in the River Teme. In those days there was no swimming pool but the town council had built two changing huts on the river bank, one for gents and another for ladies. On this particular Friday the only topic of conversation was the German invasion of Poland which made war between Britain and Germany inevitable. I can recall no sense of fear but only excitement that at long last

Hitler's bluff had been called. Little did we realise what a long and difficult task this was to be.

We were saddened, however, to think that two very nice German students who had been at school during the summer term and holiday, were immediately re-called to Germany, and that we should be fighting them in the future. This just shows how stupid international relationships can become.

However, these thoughts were soon pushed aside as we discussed what part of the Armed Forces we should like to join. As far as I was concerned, I had already decided that I would like to join the RAF as a Navigator, because I was so horrified by the idea of trench warfare similar to the first World War. At this time, however, this was purely academic as I was only sixteen and a half years old.

Ludlow in 1939 was a small market town where everyone knew everyone else, so we were soon aware that boys a few years older than us had already reported for military service. Some of them were called up under the Government Con-scription Act which compelled 21-year-olds to join up. I can recall one of our friends came on leave and looked splendid in his Guards uniform. Another chap had got his RAF wings as a Hurricane Pilot. How we looked on them with envy... A year later they were both dead, killed in action.

Throughout Saturday 2nd September there was feverish diplomatic activity between London, Paris and Berlin as the British and French Governments demanded that the German Army should withdraw from Poland otherwise a state of war would exist between Britain, France and Germany. Our main concern was that Britain and France would withdraw their guarantee of independence to Poland and once again Hitler would have "got away with it". It was not until 3rd September that Britain and France finally declared war. As far as Britain was concerned, the declaration came in a radio broadcast by the Prime Minister at 11am. He had desperately tried to settle the dispute peacefully and was devastated by his failure. He was no match for the double dealing and treacherous Hitler. Immediately after 11am the air raid sirens sounded giving warning of an impending air raid which proved to be a false alarm.

Having seen the effects in the 1930s of bombing cities in Spain and Abyssinia, it is very understandable that one of the great fears of governments in those days was that the civilian population would be heavily bombed from the beginning. The British government had therefore made plans to evacuate school children and children under school age into the country from the big cities such as Manchester, Birmingham, Liverpool, London and so on.

At the end of August 1939, when war looked imminent, Ludlow made ready to receive evacuees from the Bootle area of Liverpool. The children were sent by train from Liverpool and arrived at Ludlow in the late evening; they were supervised by helpers from Liverpool and voluntary organisations in Ludlow. They were sent round the town in lorries each child carrying a small case and gas mask. The children were billeted with the people who had volunteered to accommodate them. When the voluntary accommodation was full any remaining children were compulsorily allocated to reluctant hosts. My mother had volunteered to take two children – a boy of ten and his cousin a boy of three, luckily both turned out to be very good and well behaved.

It was about 9 pm (and therefore dark) when a knock came at the door and the Evacuation Officer plus the two children stood there. A few seconds later and we were in the room with them. My mother's first job was to find them something to eat as they had eaten little food since leaving Liverpool. We quickly found that their basic diet was "chips with everything", so I think my mother cooked egg and chips. We lived in a three bedroomed house and the two evacuees slept in the same bed in the spare bedroom. As you can imagine, we all had problems getting to sleep, especially the three year old who sobbed continuously. When we did eventually get to bed (which was very late) we were exhausted. As far as I can remember there were no guidelines issued as to how to deal with the situation – nowadays, in similar circumstances, I am sure we would be overwhelmed with Social Workers and the like.

Next morning my mother and I were down to breakfast early and wondered if it had all been a bad nightmare, but when she looked in the spare bedroom and saw these two lads fast asleep the reality came back with a bang.

It was not long before there was a knock at the door and three little lads about ten stood there enquiring if "their pal Jackie" was here, and saying that they were billeted a few doors away, and they wanted to play football.

In Liverpool, the children were obviously used to playing in the streets, so Ludlow streets soon became full of children playing football, cricket or just sitting on the pavements.

Fortunately about fifty yards from us there was the Ludlow Recreation Ground with swings and slides, so they had a great time. It was strange to hear their broad Liverpool accents (which none of us had ever heard before); it could be heard all over Ludlow.

We lived in an old, three-bedroomed house on the edge of town. Across the road was an unlimited view of open countryside stretching up to the Clee Hills and beyond. We had a garden about sixty yards long which my father cultivated very carefully and of which he was very proud. He grew quite a lot of fruit: gooseberries, raspberries and in particular I recall we had a Victoria Plum tree from which came the most delicious fruit. It did not take long for our evacuees and their friends to find the garden full of fruit... and not much longer for them to eat the lot! My father was furious, and when they had violent stomach ache he had no sympathy. I am afraid most of our friends lost their apple crops that year and many had furniture and fittings badly damaged by the evacuees – but it was all part of the wartime experience! The generally placid and slow life in Ludlow was very disrupted, although for the first time it made everyone realise how different life was in other parts of the country (for instance, most of the Liverpool children had never seen live farm animals).

In the days and weeks following the evacuations the war was very quiet and inactive and children started to return home. Our youngest visitor stayed for about three weeks and was then taken back by his parents. The boy of ten stayed with us until Christmas. He was a nice young chap and I expect he is now well into his sixties if he is still alive; he drew sketches of Hitler every day and would say to my mother, "Who is that Mrs Parsons?"

She would say, "Hitler, Jackie" and then he would stick his fist through it and laugh.

However, by Christmas he was getting very bored indeed and so he went back home. By the new year practically none of the children were left, although when bombing started in earnest six months later, Ludlow again became a centre for evacuees, but this time my mother did not take any children. She occasionally took in Airmen from the local RAF station and in 1944 took in a family from London who had left to avoid the flying bomb attacks. They remained lifelong friends.

After Christmas 1939 the weather became extremely severe all over Europe so war activity was at a very low level. During this time I was playing rugby for the school fifteen but all the matches were cancelled due to bad weather. This included several periods of freezing rain, which brought down numerous big trees and shrubs due to the weight of ice on their branches.

My Father was very keen on history and had pinned to the wall a map of the western front (i.e. the frontier between Germany and Western Europe) supplied by the *News Chronicle*, one of the big daily newspapers. Every day we listened to the news of the war in France and would move little pins around to see the armies' latest positions. This changed very slowly because the French relied almost entirely on fortification to keep the Germans out of France.

However, in April and May of 1940, Germany swept through Norway, Denmark, Holland, Belgium, France, and Luxembourg and virtually conquered the whole of Western Europe except for Great Britain. So the war had really arrived with a vengeance and this left the only means of attacking Germany from Great Britain to the RAF Bomber Command.

I was only just sixteen in 1939, still at school and taking the equivalent of 'A' levels. I had read much about the tragedies of the First World War and the dreadful conditions endured by the army in the trenches. I had already made up my mind that if I did have to join up I would volunteer to fly with the RAF, in the hope that I would either come through physically unscathed or not at all.

CHAPTER III

My First Job

In July 1940 in the last term of school the Government had asked for volunteers to attend Forestry Commission camps to help the war effort. Thinking we were all going to be lumberjacks we went to the Forestry Commission at Radnor, Mid-Wales, but in actual fact they gave us nursery weeding, a terrible job, backbreaking and most frustrating. The camp lasted about three weeks but the weather was glorious. The forestry camp was near the water reservoirs (Elan Valley) which supplied Birmingham with water. One night at about 3 am we woke to hear an aircraft flying up and down the valley. This caused great excitement because we imagined it was a German aircraft trying to bomb Birmingham's water supplies. After about half an hour it disappeared, much to our disappointment. It has to be remembered that in the late 1930s and 40s few of us had ever seen or heard an aircraft so any aerial activity aroused great interest.

Back in the 1930s and early 1940s jobs were very scarce and my Father was very keen that I should have a permanent pensionable post, so I applied to join the Birmingham Corporation. In August 1940 I received an appointment to join in September.

In September 1940 I arrived at the lodgings an aunt had found for me in Moseley, Birmingham, and joined the

Birmingham Gas Department at Windsor Street Works in Aston, a heavily industrialised suburb of Birmingham.

I was due to report for work on the first Monday in September, so I arranged to travel from Ludlow by the 3 o'clock bus on Saturday afternoon. I packed my few belongings in an old green suitcase given me by one of my aunts. Another aunt, who had a sister in Birmingham, said she would keep me company by coming with me and returning on Sunday. My Mother and Father saw me off on the bus and we made a very solemn little group. My Father looked very thoughtful and anxious and smoked cigarettes continuously, my Mother was very upset. However, it was too late to turn back and I just had to face the consequences of leaving home. When the bus pulled out of Ludlow I had a desperate feeling of homesickness, which stayed with me for the next three months (as a matter of interest the return bus fare to Birmingham was five shillings – 25p)!

Birmingham had a reputation for being a dirty industrial city and so it was in many areas, but there were also some very pleasant residential parts to the city and Moseley was one of these. Moseley had its own golf course and many tree lined avenues which were very attractive indeed. However to get to Windsor Street Gas Works involved about a seven mile bus journey. So on the Monday morning I started off in plenty of time and after a ten minute walk to the bus stop, joined a long queue of people. The bus took me to the city centre where I had to change, the total return bus fare to Aston and back was 3p on a 'workman's ticket'! The bus journey itself was a revelation to me, we stood shoulder to shoulder on a packed bus and if you wanted a guaranteed seat you went upstairs where smoking was permitted. I was a non-smoker and, I found the atmosphere unbelievably thick because most people smoked in those days and the top part of the bus rattled to the sound of smokers coughing. I changed buses in the city centre and took the short journey from the city centre into Aston.

Coming from Ludlow with its green grass and green trees, the river Teme and the fresh air, there could not have been a bigger contrast with Aston. There were all terraced houses many of which were back to back and built round small courtyards which had common toilets and washrooms for several houses. Many of the houses were in a state of decay and would be rightly described as slums (they were cleared after the war for rebuilding where not already demolished by bombing).

The smells from the area were many and varied: from the gasworks came the smell of coal gas, sulphur and tar, and the smell of beer from Ansells Brewery mixed with the smell of HP sauce from another nearby factory. In the middle of these fragrant surroundings, I reported for work on Monday morning.

One of the first things I noticed when I started work was the punctuality with which everyone seemed to travel. Most of the men in the road where I lodged had administrative jobs in the city so that at a certain time every morning the front door would open and out would emerge a smartly dressed man in a dark suit, trilby hat, umbrella (rolled up) and either wearing or carrying a mackintosh. This was typical of my next-door neighbour who was a cashier in the Britannic Assurance Offices in Birmingham. He was about 38 years old and lived with his wife, mother-in-law and two boys, aged seven and six months (an extremely nice family). He was unfit for military service because of poor eyesight – he had to wear very heavily lensed spectacles. His timing was as accurate as a clock in that he left home at exactly 8:05 every morning, and with exactly the same number of strides reached the bus stop where he met exactly the same number of people. To reach my Gas Office on time, I should have caught the same bus as him, but I was usually running to catch him up, after realising I was late when he passed our dining room windows!

Sometimes I did catch him up and exchanged a few pleasantries. I would ask him how he had fared at work the previous day. Quite often he would say, "I didn't get home until 9 pm last night. We were a shilling (5p) out in our cash balance so we had to stay until we found it."

I thought to myself, 'What a rotten job,' but his was considered a prestigious occupation in those days.

After about a month of travelling on the bus I got very fed up and decided to send for my bike. My colleagues in the Gas Office gave me a short cut route from Moseley to Aston which only took about half an hour if all went well. It was not a very pleasant route to take as I had to cycle through an area which was heavily industrialised. It was subjected to very heavy bombing and to cycle through this area the morning after an air raid was quite an experience – there were smouldering fires, warning signs because of unexploded bombs and bomb craters everywhere. It sometimes took one and a half hours to make what should have been a half-hour journey.

In those days there was no 'Clean Air Act' and in the winter the industrial atmosphere produced fogs when visibility would be less than five yards and all traffic would come to a complete halt.

I was given the job of a very junior clerk in the Time Office, which consisted of mainly answering the telephone, a few clerical jobs and running messages. A far cry from doing A-level History! The office itself was very old and dirty and lit with the old-fashioned gas lights, so the atmosphere was always very stuffy, especially when the old coke fire was burning.

When I turned up at the office on the first day I had a nice new suit, clean shirt, tie and a new coat. It only took a little while to realise that the atmosphere penetrated clothing, as within two days my shirts and underclothes were black, so I needed frequent baths, and a change of underclothes two or three times a week.

There were about ten male clerks (no women were employed), all concerned with time being worked by employees in order to pay the wages. On many occasions there were violent disputes between the clerks and the employees over hours worked. Even in those days there were coloured employees working in the gas works and it was not unusual on a Friday to find an Indian or Pakistani threatening the chief Time Keeper with violence.

The Windsor Street Gas Works in Aston was one of four huge gas works in the city and they employed maintenance gasholder gangs to look after the gasholders. These gangs used to collect their pay on a Friday but sometimes if they were at a works other than Windsor Street they would ring up and ask for their pay to be sent wherever they were. Sometimes I was given the job of taking the packets to them. On one occasion I was asked to take the gas holder gang's pay to Washwood Heath Gas Works. I took these ten packets by bus and made my way there, I asked the gatekeeper where the gang was, and he said they were at the bottom of the gasholder and could I take the pay to them. I had no alternative but to walk over the top of the gasholder (which was empty) to a small hole in the middle from which poked a ladder. I looked through the hole and saw a drop of about two hundred feet with the ladder going to the floor. The gang were at the bottom of the ladder and shouted "bring the money down". With my heart in my boots I got onto the ladder and climbed down to give them their money. They were all in fits of laughter, especially as they knew I had to climb up again. It was with a great sense of relief that I got out and I was pleased not to have to do this job again!

One of the problems of getting on the bus, especially in the dark, was finding out where it was going, because in the blackout it was difficult to see anything. There were only small lights in the bus, and the destination numbers had been dimmed so it was hard to know whether you were even on the right bus. Of course the blackout was an important part of the defence against air attack. There were air raid wardens patrolling the streets every night. They would shout, 'put that light out' if they saw any sign of light. Failure to obey their instructions could mean appearing in court and facing substantial fines. The station signs and road signs were removed, to ensure that if there was an invasion the Germans would not have any signposts telling them where they were.

Another important civil defence against air attack was the formation of fire watching teams. In every road there would be three to four teams working voluntary shifts during the night keeping watch. In the event of air attack incendiaries would always be dropped and these could penetrate into houses (lofts) and set them alight without the occupants knowing. So fire watching was vital protection.

I had only been in my new digs for a week when I was approached to join one of the fire watching teams, which I did. During the night watch we would often put out loft fires caused by incendiaries using stirrup pumps or buckets of sand. We used to patrol in pairs and talk to pass the time, I remember talking to one man about cricket to pass the night away. It was cold and uncofortable in the winter, but it was a very successful part of air defence. Protection against air attack was also provided by the steel 'Anderson' shelters constructed in the gardens and usually shared by two houses. They would stand anything except a direct hit and therefore saved many lives. It was not unusual for people to go into the shelters from about six at night until six in the morning because the German method was to have very long raids to keep defences alert all night. The atmosphere in the shelter was very stuffy and claustrophobic, but we would sing songs, make pots and pots of tea and be very amenable to each other. Later in the war the indoor 'Morrison' shelter was introduced. These steel 'table' shelters were said to be strong enough to withstand a direct hit. Even if the building collapsed, the occupants would be safe underneath. These were an eyesore, filled up the whole lounge and were very difficult to crawl under – but again they saved lives.

The first night I was in Birmingham there was a twelve hour raid and although Moseley was only a suburb it was on the direct flight from France whence the bombers came to bomb the BSA, GEC, and all main arms factories in Birmingham. It was not unusual for aircraft to drop bombs before the main targets were reached. As the anti-aircraft guns tried to prevent the bombers reaching the main target we were well showered in Moseley with incendiaries and bombs. I think in the first three months I was in Birmingham until about December I do not think there were many nights where there was not an air-raid.

The experience of an air raid is unique – a mixture of fear and excitement, especially for a teenager like me. We could take stock of the weather and forecast fairly accurately whether a raid was likely to take place that night (a clear moonlit night was almost certain to produce an air raid). At about 6.30pm the warning sirens would start (a shrill wailing sound). This would be followed by an hour of silence after which the steady drone of approaching aircraft would be heard. The sky would be lit up by searchlights looking for the raiders followed by the crashes of the anti aircraft guns firing. High explosives and incendiaries would be dropped and the high explosive bombs would whistle as they fell (it was always said that you never heard the bomb that hit you)!

Much damage was caused in these bombing attacks, but people went to work tired but nevertheless, carried on. Often it took a long time to get to work as buses had to be diverted to avoid new bomb damage caused by the previous night's raids. In one such raid I remember someone shouting "Mind out Eileen, there's some incendiaries falling!" The girl was crossing from one side of the road to the other and turned out to be the girl I later met at a dance and in 1944 married. That was fifty six years ago and was the best thing that ever happened to me! So Hitler did me some good after all!

An incident that occurred during one of the heavy November raids is worth noting. About a mile from where I lived was Swanhurst Park, where an anti aircraft battery was stationed which used to fire at the German aircraft as they flew overhead. The noise when they fired was tremendous. It shook doors and windows violently. On this occasion after one of these salvos of anti aircraft shells had been sent hurtling into the sky, there was a noise from one of the aircraft as though it had been hit. It sounded in great difficulty and in order to stay in the air the pilot decided to jettison all his bombs. So we were showered with incendiaries and high explosives. St Agnes church about a mile away was demolished, as were several houses around. A small high explosive landed about 30 yards from where we lived and damaged doors and windows. A large high explosive would have probably killed or injured us.

By the beginning of 1941, Germany was thinking of attacking Russia rather than Great Britain, so gradually the air raids subsided. This was a relief and life became more normal.

Eileen and I went to the pictures or dancing. In the meantime, I was eighteen years old and I joined the Home Guard (Dad's Army!) whose job it was to guard the gas works in Aston. It was quite an experience, as we had to patrol at night around the gasworks and railway lines. This was quite dangerous in case one fell over the machines and equipment in the blackout.

CHAPTER IV

Trainee Navigator

In 1941 there was no sign of the war ending and the papers were full of advertisements for air crew. So at eighteen and a half I joined the RAF to train as a navigator. The only way to get into flying duties was by volunteering. I had to get special permission from my employer to do this. In November 1941 I went along to the Air Crew recruiting offices in Dale End, Birmingham and said I would like to fly, which was a bit bold because at this time I had hardly seen any aircraft let alone flown in one! There were thousands of others volunteering, attracted by the glamorous adverts, the uniforms and wings and of course the flying. Little did we know what was waiting for us ahead.

Dale End accepted me for air crew after medicals which were very strict. There were also strict educational tests before you could be passed for training. One of the physical tests which was particularly daunting was to hold up a column of mercury for 90 seconds without breathing in, which meant you had to hold your breath. Many applicants failed to do this, so I made sure I did not fail by practising holding my breath for two minutes at a time so that when I came to the RAF test I passed without any problems. There were so many people accepted that I joined a waiting list for training. I was put on 5 months deferred service which meant

I kept thinking they had forgotten about me; this shows how stupid you can be. I used to write to them asking when I was going to be called up and my mother use to say, they won't forget you, which of course they didn't, and sure enough I received my instructions to join in June 1942 by reporting to Lords cricket ground in London which was the aircrew reception centre.

I can remember Father, Mother and Eileen my girlfriend coming to see me off on the platform at Birmingham, New Street, Station. My father was puffing on his cigarette as usual saying "I think you will be gone for two years." In the end I was gone for nearly five.

It was a strange feeling getting on the train with my little suitcase. I sat in the corner of the carriage as the train pulled out of New Street Station, Birmingham and all sorts of things flashed through my mind. The most powerful was a feeling of apprehension that, in reality, flying might not be as glamorous as it appeared from Civvy Street, but this was coupled with a sense of great excitement, because I was on my way to Lord's, the most famous cricket ground in the world (both, then and now).

From the age of ten I had been a cricket fanatic. I knew by heart all the famous players and I listened to every radio broadcast. When I was twelve I found I had the knack, an unusual knack, of spinning the cricket ball from the leg-side, so I played regularly for the school eleven team, and for the Ludlow and South Shropshire cricket club. When the train pulled into London Euston, I anxiously looked around to see if there were any lads my age carrying a small suitcase, but there did not appear to be anybody. I made my way to the Underground and took the train to Swiss Cottage, the tube station nearest to Lord's. Suddenly I was surrounded by hundreds of other young chaps making their way to the main gates of the famous Cricket Ground. We showed our call-up papers and were ticked off on a list – I was 'in'!

We were told to sit down on one of the seats in the ground and to wait until we were called. After about a two hour wait, around forty of us were called to the 'Long Room', which housed all the famous photographs. We were in the charge of a sergeant and a corporal, and formed up in threes. After a few words of introduction, the sergeant told us to prepare for a Medical Examination.

"Now lads," he said, "I want you to take all your clothes off, including your socks and shoes, and put them in a neat pile at the back of the room, and remember which is yours! After you have done that, line up in threes."

When we were ready the Medical officer walked up and down the line to make sure we were free from obvious infection. This was called an 'FFI' and was only the first of many such inspections we would be subjected to in the following year. On this first occasion when it was all new, most of us paled with embarrassment, but we very quickly realised that an order is something you carry out without question. After the inspection we were handed over to the corporal.

At the outbreak of war, many professional sportsmen had joined the war as drill or physical training instructors. Our Corporal was a professional footballer who played Centre

Forward for Luton Town in the Second Division. It was stated that he had scored ten goals in one game, hence his nickname 'Ten Goal Joe Payne'. He was a nice man who looked after us well. He formed us again in threes and marched us off to our billet in the most luxurious part of London – around Regent's Park. The name of the flat I was billeted in was Stockleigh Hall, a very desirable residence! There were three airman to each flat, giving us plenty of space. We ate all our meals in the Regent's Park Zoo Cafeteria.

Most of the three weeks I spent in London was spent in getting kitted out in RAF uniform. We found that the RAF made a distinction between trainee air-crew and the rest. We wore a white flash in our caps and wore shoes instead of boots and at night we had sheets to sleep in, not just blankets.

The most dreaded day was one in which we joined a long queue to have inoculations. It was not unusual for men to pass out when they saw four doctors waiting with the needles. After this we were allowed 24 hours complete rest.

On the whole, apart from the injections, it was a most pleasant three weeks. We usually finished duty about 5 o'clock and the weekends were free, so we were able to have a look round London, where we had not been before, so we enjoyed visiting the cinema and watching cricket.

After 3 weeks in London we were posted to our first RAF Station. Imagine my surprise when I found it was to my home town of Ludlow in Shropshire! I remember my Father telling me that he had heard rumours that the RAF was to open a camp about 2 miles out of Ludlow on the Hereford road. This rumour unlike most of them was well founded and so several hundred trainee aircrew arrived at Ludlow station in July 1942. The extraordinary thing about this was that we actually built the camp when we got there. Water supplies had been fixed and road building had started, but we had to erect tents, build toilets etc.

When I was accepted for aircrew training I (and everyone else) had a very nice welcoming letter. Effectively this said that we were the 'cream' of the country and we should be proud of our selection. In those days the most popular hairdressing was Brylcreem and national advertisements showed top sporting and film stars dressed in aircrew uniform with hair treated with Brylcreem! We were soon called 'The Brylcreem Boys' and this, together with our distinguishing white flash in our caps, led many people to think we were a bunch of softies.

I have often wondered why we should as trainee aircrew start our careers as camp builders. Firstly, there was a blockage in the Air Training Scheme because of the intake of larger numbers and Ludlow relieved the blockage and gave us something useful to do. Secondly, it knocked any feelings of arrogance out of us and although we were aircrew trainees we could still be called to do the most basic jobs.

We formed up in threes outside Ludlow station and marched through the centre of the town to the camp. The local people had turned out in force to welcome us and it seemed strange to me that I recognised most of them, including my Father and Mother, who had joined the crowd. The campsite was literally fields and we were divided into groups in the charge of a sergeant who we quickly nicknamed 'Tiny'. He was a huge man, I would guess about six foot four inches tall, very brown with a splendid tan and obviously very fit. I think he had worked in road building before the war and he told us that with our help we would build roads together. This was his job at the camp. There was no shortage of road building materials from the Clee Hill granite quarries nearby and no shortage of sledgehammers and wheelbarrows!

We slept under canvas about six to a tent and although in many circumstances we would have regarded it as uncomfortable, after a day's road building we were so tired we could have slept anywhere. Every morning at 7am we would hear this huge roar.

"Wakey Wakey! I want all you men on the road at 8:15!"

And so to another day of stone breaking...

From time to time I did manage to slip home to see my parents and my girlfriend Eileen who travelled to Ludlow from Birmingham at the weekends. My Grandmother and my Aunt organised a Forces canteen, which was very good, but I am afraid I was so tired I was not much company for anyone.

Although this was a million miles away from aircrew training I suppose the three weeks did us some good in raising our physical fitness but it took some weeks for the blisters to heal and my backache to disappear.

In December 1941 America joined the war against Germany. Several million US Troops were based in the UK in 1944 in preparation for the invasion of Europe. The Ludlow RAF camp built by us trainee aircrew accommodated many thousand Americans so I suppose we did some good after all.

After three weeks in Ludlow, about two hundred of us were posted to the Initial Training Wing at Aberystwyth. There were about ten such 'wings' operating in different parts of the country, mostly sea-side resorts, although there were a few in towns like Stratford-on Avon, and Cambridge. This really was the beginning of Aircrew Training.

It was a tough three months course, with a detailed exam at the end. Failure to pass this examination meant that you were rejected for Aircrew. This unfortunately, happened to quite a few.

When the train arrived at Aberystwyth, we were met by a formidable bunch of NCOs (Sergeants and Corporals). We were told to form up outside the station and were then marched down the main street to the promenade. I remember that it was a glorious sunny day in August and Aberystwyth was full of holidaymakers. We lined up on the promenade under the gaze of the locals and holidaymakers and the senior NCO read our names from a list, which divided us into squadrons and flight numbers. A sergeant and two corporals wew assigned to each flight. Our sergeant was named Johnson. He was a short man with bright red hair. He had joined the RAF in 1935, well before the war and resented new recruits being promoted faster than he had been in peacetime. Under his direction and the Corporal's, we were marched to our billet, which was a holiday hotel on the seafront and very comfortable. There were three airmen to each room, which had a bathroom adjoining. My two companions were from Yorkshire and Northumberland and luckily the three of us got on very well together. After we had unloaded our kit bags we were told to parade on the promenade where Sergeant Johnson laid down the rules for the next three months. He said he was an iron disciplinarian bastard and if we failed to follow his rules we would be in serious trouble! We were issued with a timetable for the three months, similar to a school timetable. Mixed up with studying academic subjects, were periods for foot drill, drill with a rifle and physical training. Time was also allowed for billet and kit inspection, which was where Sergeant Johnson and his Corporal took over.

We marched up and down that promenade until we were exhausted, especially so, as we marched 140 paces to the minute, which was very fast indeed. If we did not get it right in the daytime, he marched us back in the evening. He had further sources of power with his inspection. The billet was inspected every day to see that it was all in good shape – beds made up to perfection, bathrooms spotless, and not any dust on the tops of door jambs and furniture etc, and every month there was a kit inspection. At the beginning, they had an easy job in catching us out, and many of us were confined to our billet as a punishment, but we gradually got wise to what they wanted us to do, so life became more bearable.

Physical training included games and cross country running, and I really enjoyed playing cricket for the Squadron. The cross-country running was particularly formidable, it consisted of running along the promenade and up the steep Constitution Hill at the end, and a further four miles of country beyond Aberystwyth.

Apart from the academic side, it proved to be a very tough physical course, and I had never been so fit, before and since those days, in the Autumn of 1942.

Most of the lecturers had previously taught in Universities and so they were highly qualified. I cannot remember all the subjects we studied but they included the theory of flight, elementary engines, meteorology and navigation. In addition we learned Morse Code, signalling with an Aldis Lamp, aircraft recognition and the rudiments of health and hygiene. As you can see, this was a very comprehensive training programme, and I was very glad to pass the exams finally.

When I joined the RAF, we were all given the rank of AC2 – the lowest form of life in the Airforce. By passing this exam I became a LAC which is a Leading Aircraftsman, and my pay was seven shillings (i.e. thirty five pence) per day.

It was now November 1942, and again there was a huge blockage in training courses, so having taken a week's leave I was posted to a transit camp at Heaton Park, Manchester, to await the next stage.

The majority of training for pilots and navigators took place in the flying schools in Canada and South Africa, so the trainees who had passed their ITW exams were sent to Heaton Park where they were formed into overseas drafts before being sent to the port in Glasgow. I had visited Heaton Park before the war – we had friends at Middleton, just outside Manchester, and when we visited them in 1937, they insisted on taking us to this huge park. In the war it was commandeered by the RAF and although some buildings were erected in the park, the majority of Aircrew trainees were billeted in private houses nearby. I was billeted with a middle-aged Jewish couple, their sole lodger, and although they were very kind to me, I felt rather lonely. Hitherto, I had always had company since joining the RAF. However, I soon made friends with a few RAF men who were billeted a few doors away. We used to go together to morning parade at 9am. After we had been checked off on parade there was literally nothing to do, which was very boring, and soon the keenness and enthusiasm we had acquired at ITW disappeared. As we marched into the camp in the morning the tannoy used to blast out the tune 'Fall in and Fly' – a big joke, as none of us thought we would ever get to fly.

Sometimes I got a weekend pass to go home. If I did not get a pass I would go home anyway and risk being picked up by the RAF police who patrolled big stations like Manchester and Birmingham, looking for airmen without a pass. After a while I became skilled at dodging them, so did others. Four weeks passed and I was sent to another transit camp at Bridgnorth. It was now January 1943, when a group of us were told to get our kit packed ready to move out the following morning. No one gave us any indication where we were going, so we assumed it to be an overseas draft.

We assembled on Bridgnorth station at 8am in the middle of a snowstorm, and boarded a special coach reserved for the RAF which was attached to the ordinary train. Then began the most extraordinary journey. We went from Bridgnorth to Shrewsbury to Chester then to Manchester, from there to Huddersfield, on to Leeds, then to York and finally ended up at Scarborough at 1:00 am – a 17-hour journey! Nobody told us where we were going, or why, and we were astonished as our carriage was shunted from train to train at these various stations. The truth finally emerged at Scarborough, where three motor coaches were waiting, with RAF men with the RAF Regiment insignia on their uniform. The RAF Regiment were trained like the Army and their job was to guard airfields against enemy ground attack. We suddenly realised that we were with the RAF Regiment. They informed us we were on a three week training course. What a far cry it was from flying – another time waster!

The training centre was at Filey, between Scarborough and Bridlington. We climbed aboard the coaches and off we went to Filey. It was a bitterly cold night with an icy cold wind coming from the North sea. We were billeted in commandeered boarding houses on a hill overlooking the sea. Some of the windows were missing, possibly by enemy action, it was freezing cold, and we went to bed in our greatcoats and everything we could get our hands on. Even today I shudder at the thought of Filey!

The RAF Regiment trainers had already decided they were going to give these soft Aircrews a tough time, which in fact they did. We did bayonet practice, rifle shooting, attacking bogus enemies on Filey golf course at 1am and then there was marching, marching and yet more marching. We kept up with the training schedule, in spite of all their efforts to defeat us. I was glad, Sergeant Johnson and his Corporals had been so strict at Aberystwyth.

One day, we were taken to a demonstration by the RAF Regiment at Butlins Holiday Camp in Filey. Two of the RAF

Regiment were detailed to attack a hill overlooking the sea, they were fully kitted out, and as they made their way across the land towards the hill, there was a sudden burst of machine gun fire. The ground was being kicked up just behind these men, and they climbed the hill at a very rapid pace as the gunfire followed them. Open mouthed we asked what was going on. We were told that they always used live ammunition in training, as it made for more realism!

As we marched back into Filey from Butlin's (about two miles) rumours quickly spread that there was to be another exercise the following day and that some of us may be involved. This made us very worried. It was not unusual for servicemen to be killed during training; for example, Royal Navy ships had been accidentally bombed by the RAF and RAF aircraft had been accidentally shot down by the Royal Navy, so if a few trainee Air Crew were shot by the RAF Regiment during training it would not cause much upset. Fortunately it was just a rumour; next day we resumed our normal rifle drill and patrols over Filey golf course.

About the middle of February 1943 while still wasting time at Heaton Park. I had managed to get a week-end pass to visit my girlfriend Eileen in Birmingham. On the Sunday I suddenly began to feel very hot, as though running a temperature with influenza. As the day progressed I became steadily worse. The RAF rule was that if you were taken ill on leave you had to contact the nearest RAF station, where there were always medical facilities. In my deteriorating condition we had to inform RAF Wythall (about six miles outside Birmingham) and they sent an ambulance to pick me up.

I was seen immediately by the MO who, having taken my temperature, diagnosed influenza and ordered me to bed in the sick bay. At this time I noticed some soreness in my right side. Before joining the RAF, I had had several minor attacks of colitis, which disappeared with treatment, so when I had a repeat of the symptoms I disregarded them. With a struggle I managed to get some sleep but I woke at around 5am and felt very ill. My right side had stiffened and became badly swollen. I called the medical orderly to have a look at me. He felt my side, went pale, and called the MO, who immediately revised his diagnosis of 'flu' to a possibility of peritonitis and rang the Queen Elizabeth Hospital in Birmingham to arrange for my immediate transfer as an emergency.

The Queen Elizabeth Hospital was about ten miles from RAF Wythall and I recall little about the journey. I must have been in a semi-coma and I remember feeling as though my mind had left my body and that I was watching someone else lying on a stretcher, not recognising it as myself. I must have felt that I was unlikely to recover.

When I arrived at the Queen Elizabeth (which had only been opened a few years earlier) I was examined by a young surgeon who had no hesitation in ordering an emergency operation, which he performed using a lumbar puncture to freeze the bottom half of the body. Apparently there was too much risk of sickness from a general anaesthetic and that would have been disastrous.

I can still remember the theatre staff moving around me because of course I was completely conscious. The operation seemed endless and at the end the surgeon said how lucky I was. He said, "We found an abscess in your appendix the size of a Jaffa orange. In a few hours it would have burst and then I'm afraid it would have been too late. We have had to put a rubber tube into the abscess to drain it. We could not see your appendix to take it out. That will require a separate operation in six months or so." I still carry a huge scar.

After the operation, I was in the Queen Elizabeth for about ten days. I was in a military ward which had some army chaps who had been in North Africa and had some bad injuries caused by shrapnel from bombs dropped by German 'Stuka' Dive Bombers which they said were absolutely terrifying. There was however one amusing incident in the ward, one of the army chaps said he was going to try to get a discharge on medical grounds and complained to the Medical Staff that he had lost all feelling in his arms and hands. It looked as if he was going to be successful until a brain consultant was brought in. In front of us all, he examined this chap, touching various parts of his hand with a pen and asking for comments as to whether he had any feeling. After a short while the consultant thoroughly confused him. He was saying he had feeling where he could not have in the alleged complaint and vice versa. He ended up by being told off for time wasting and did not get his discharge ticket, in fact he was lucky to escape being put on a charge.

After a week in hospital I felt much better and was sent to a military convalescent home at Lichfield. All this time I had wonderful support from Eileen and from my Mother and Father who visited me regularly and kept me feeling cheerful.

After convalescence, I reported back to the RAF at Heaton Park and I was sent to an RAF Consultant at Wilmslow - a very nice place. He decided I was still not fully fit and ordered me to have ten days in the RAF convalescent home hotel commandeered by the RAF in South Shore Blackpool. By this time I was feeling very much better especially when Eileen came to Blackpool for a few days. In spite of the war the Pleasure Beach was in full swing and we had a fabulous time there and went on the Big Dipper (amongst other things). Happy Days! All in all I was out of action for about two months, before I was fit enough to resume duties.

Once more I returned to Manchester, this time there was better news. Apparently, the construction of an Air Field at Bishops Court near Ardglass, Northern Ireland was well underway and was advanced enough to allow the Avro Anson to 'take off' from there. This was an Aircraft which was used to train Navigators. It had, therefore, been decided to set up ground navigators courses in Bridgnorth, followed by flying training in Northern Ireland. I found I was one of the lucky ones to be on the first course.

After a few days on this course at Bridgnorth all the frustration and boredom of the previous six months had disappeared. The course was very intensive, the main subject being the theory of Air Navigation was based on 'dead reckoning'; the required track from A to B was drawn on a map, the compass course to fly to achieve this track was calculated by using the wind direction and speed, and all this information was plotted on to the same map. As far as the weather was concerned we were taught all about cloud formation, weather fronts, fog. etc. I have not flown since the war but I have no doubt that the weather is still a very important factor in flying today, even though modern aircraft can fly above the weather and even land in thick fog with sophisticated instruments. In the 1940s there was no way that aircraft could fly above the weather – you had to fly under it, round it, or through it, so knowledge, particularly about cloud formations and their inherent dangers, was vital.

We were also taught how to navigate by the stars. If you take into account aircraft recognition and ship recognition, you can see, there was no time to spare, we were continually being told that theory would be translated into practice when we joined the flying school in Northern Ireland, and so the greater knowledge we had, could save our lives.

We had one day a week off and because Bridgnorth was only seventeen miles from Ludlow I used to get home for the day. At the end of the course there were another set of detailed examinations to pass. In early August 1943 I, together with thirty others who had passed the exam found ourselves on the night train to Stranraer. The Scottish port from which the ferries sailed to Larne in Northern Ireland. It was a beautiful sunny morning and the sea was like a millpond. It was a most enjoyable crossing which took about two hours. We then travelled by train to Belfast where we changed trains on to the County Down Railway. Our first glimpse of Belfast showed the policemen carrying guns, as though they were anticipating trouble, even in those days. The County Down Railway was rather a quaint little train of which we had plenty of experience over the following months. The nearest station to the camp at Bishops Court was Ardglass about forty miles south of Belfast. Every Saturday the camp almost closed down. A special train was organised for us to spend the day in Belfast where we enjoyed ourselves. There was much more choice of food in cafes and goods to buy in the shops. Also, good films to see at the 'pictures' as it was called.

The return journey, late on a Saturday night, was always an experience. The final approach to Ardglass was a steep hill and the engine was not strong enough to pull the whole train, which had to be divided into three sections. One by one, each section of four coaches was hauled to the top of the hill, to the cheers of the airmen within when it arrived at the top, where the train was joined together again. This process used to take about one and a half hours. It was rumoured that sometimes the engine would run out of fuel and that the passengers would help by collecting wood at the side of the lines. Nothing would have surprised me.

Bishops Court Aerodrome was only a few miles from Ardglass and so being taken by lorry from the station took a matter of thirty minutes. The Aerodrome was situated right on the coast and so it was possible to walk to the beach and bathe in the sea although the Irish sea was too cold for this, even in summer. From the Aerodrome there were some beautiful views, especially of the Mourne Mountains which come down to the sea about 30 miles away, although they were frequently covered by low cloud. We were accommodated in wooden huts, about twenty to each hut and were quite comfortable.

The first few days were spent explaining how the course was going to be run. It was to last three months, and at the end of that time, the successful airmen would receive the Navigators Beret and Sergeants Stripes.

There were still going to be ground lectures and exercises, but the main emphasis was to be on flying Navigators Training. We were divided into pairs who would work together while flying, one man would be the first navigator and calculate the courses to fly, and maintain the record (log) of the flight. The second man would map read from the nose of the aircraft. His duties would be alternated with the first airman.

The crew consisted of: the pilot instructor who was captain of the aircraft and was familiar with the training routes to be flown; the fully qualified 'wireless operator' responsible for communication with the ground wireless stations; two trainee navigators; one or two trainee wireless operators.

We flew in an Avro Anson Aircraft at about 3,000 to 5,000 feet, at a cruising speed of 120 miles per hour – only about the speed of one of today's fast cars!

The Anson had been built in the 1930s and the undercarriage did not retract automatically. It was the job of the trainee navigator to wind it up and down manually after 'take off' and on landing. What a rotten job!

To operate the wireless, it was necessary to unwind a long trailing aerial once the aircraft was airborne, and had achieved a reasonable height. This was operated by the trainee wireless operator.

There were about twelve pilot instructors on the course and we could find ourselves flying with anyone of them. On the 5th August 1943, the whole course was instructed to report to the briefing room where we were given details of our first flight. My co-navigator, Tony Ward from Bristol and I were told to fly with Flight Sergeant McLemon. As we walked outside to the aircraft, we felt a strong mixture of apprehension and excitement. After the usual cockpit checks we became airborne for the first time at 9.30 am on a glorious cloudless day. It was fascinating to leave the runway, and to see the hedges and trees slipping away below. As we climbed to a height of 2,000 feet there were some brilliant views over the Northern Ireland coastline and countryside. This first trip only lasted one hour and half to give us our first experience together with a little map-reading.

Before flying, I had been concerned, as had most others, about the feeling of height and the possibility of air sickness. Neither of these problems occurred. One trainee, however, suffered so badly from air sickness he was forced to give up flying. We were all feeling very sorry about this, especially so, as he had been so keen to fly.

After the initial flight on 5th August, we flew regularly in training exercises. A typical exercise was to fly from base to Chicken Rock Lighthouse, at the southern tip of the Isle of Man, to Bardsey Island in Wales, then to South Stack Lighthouse near Holyhead, and then back to base. In practice, we rarely flew exactly the same flight twice.

We would fly over the Lake District, Southern Scotland and North Wales. When we were being given ground lectures, we were told how critically important it was to keep checking the wind strength and direction. For example, if you were flying from Belfast to Liverpool, it was fairly straightforward to join these two places together on a navigator's map, and to calculate the angle. If you tried to fly this angle by a compass, and the wind was from a southerly direction, you would end up at Blackpool and not Liverpool, having been blown 'off course' by the wind. So, in calculating the compass course, the wind has to be taken into account. It was the navigator's job to do this, and to be continually checking the calculations. If you look at any of today's weather maps, they show the variable speed and direction of the wind, which can vary greatly over a short distance. Just imagine the difficulty doing this in the 1940s with very little information available.

These difficulties were brought home to us with great force one night in September when we were sent on a training exercise at night, which included flying about 15 miles from Snowdon. On our return, one of our aircraft was missing, which caused great anxiety. Our worst fears were confirmed early next morning by the news that the crashed aircraft had been found near the summit of Snowdon. There were no survivors. They were all our friends, and we felt their loss very keenly, but they were only the first of many friends to be lost during the following two and a half years. The only way to keep flying was to adopt a very hardened attitude; we all realised only too well that our next flight could be our last. Flying in the RAF was known as 'dicing with death' and this saying was very true. The threat of crashing certainly gave you the incentive to work with greater precision!

By the end of October 1943 I had completed 75 hours of daylight flying, and 25 hours at night. I had much sympathy with the pilot instructors who had become pilots in the hope of flying in action on fighters or bombers. Instead of which, they were doing the boring job of training navigators. One pilot instructor, a Canadian, was so bored that when we were flying over the sea, he would often decide to do some 'low flying'. This was terrifying because we felt that at any moment we would crash. (I had a schoolfriend who was a pilot, training navigators, who was killed in this way along with all the trainees.)

On 5 November 1943 I passed out as a fully qualified navigator. It was an excellent course, and, if you look at the map of the Irish sea and the neighbouring country, you will see the mountains of the Lake District, Wales, Isle of Man and Ireland provided us with plenty of good experience.

Certificates of Qualification.

(to be filled in as appropriate)

1. This is to certify that 1582516. LAC. PARSONS.

   has qualified as AIR NAVIGATOR.

   with effect from 5.11.43. Sgd J.R. Wright. S/c

   Date 4.11.43. Unit 7. A.O.S.

2. This is to certify that _____

   has qualified as _____

   with effect from _____ Sgd _____

   Date _____ Unit _____

3. This is to certify that _____

   has qualified as _____

   with effect from _____ Sgd _____

   Date _____ Unit _____

4. This is to certify that _____

   has qualified as _____

   with effect from _____ Sgd _____

   Date _____ Unit _____

CHAPTER V

Joining a Bomber Crew

On the 5th November 1943 I became a qualified Navigator, just over sixteen months after joining the RAF in June 1942. About half this time was spent on actual training, the remainder just waiting about. Navigators who trained in Canada and South Africa found they needed supplementary help after returning to the UK because conditions flying overseas were so different from European flying (i.e. the weather over there was more stable and the towns and railway lines were much easier to identify). We found that training in European conditions was a great advantage.

My next move was to be sent home to Ludlow on indefinite leave to await posting to an operational training unit – this is where newly qualified Pilots, Navigators, Bomb Aimers, Wireless Operators and Gunners were sent to form crews whose subsequent training would eventually enable the crew to fly a Lancaster Bomber anywhere over Europe. After two weeks leave I received a telegram to join the OTU at Desborough in Northamptonshire.

When I arrived there I found that the Airfield was about five miles from the town and had only been built 18 months ago and consisted of temporary buildings (Nissen huts). The Nissen hut was quick and easy to construct with its concrete floor, corrugated sides and ceiling shaped like an arch. There were two or three stoves spread out along the centre and accommodated about thirty men to each hut. These huts were bitterly cold during winter, unless you could keep warm by the stove, and equally hot during the summer months. Most of the year the ground round these concrete paths was churned up mud. In other words, it was the most uncomfortable place I had found myself in so far.

Two days after our arrival, a meeting was called of all the new airmen. After a few words of introduction we were told to form ourselves into crews as best we could. This was not an easy task amongst complete strangers, but I remember a 21 year old Canadian pilot called Ed. We got on well and decided to crew together; slowly, others joined us and we ended up a 'six man' crew. Before flying training commenced, we were scheduled to have two weeks ground training.

In the weeks before I went to Desborough I had started to experience some discomfort in the area of my appendix which steadily became worse. I reported sick at and was immediately sent to the RAF hospital at Ely where they removed my appendix. I had ten days in hospital followed by five weeks at a convalescent home in Ely, but my main memory of this period is of the Burns Unit at the hospital where there were a number of aircrew who had been badly burned after crashing during training. Although the doctors were doing a marvellous job with plastic surgery, seeing them was very upsetting and did nothing to quell my anxieties about the future. I could soon be in the same condition.

Early in January 1944 I reported back to Desborough fit for duty but I found that my former crew had been given a replacement Navigator and had left Desborough for the next stage in training, so I joined with another crew who were short of a Navigator.

At this time I had developed a severe head cold which went to my chest so I was not really fit to fly, but fearful that I might be accused of malingering after having had so much time off sick already, I carried on. My condition became rapidly worse and I could hardly breathe. The station medical officer was summoned and his diagnosis was that one of my lungs had collapsed, so once again I was sent to RAF Hospital – this time at Halton near Aylesbury – where I spent about eight weeks. My ward was full of men with chest infections, most of whom were discharged back to civilian life, being declared unfit for further service in the RAF. Fortunately, I made a complete recovery and once again returned to Desborough to resume training.

At the end of March 1944 I joined yet another crew who had lost their navigator through illness. I stayed with this crew until the end of the war. They were:

Graham (Mac) Baxter	Pilot	age 21
Leslie Parsons	Navigator	age 21
Algy Smith	Bomb Aimer	age 27
George Brooker	Wireless operator	age 21
Frank Ramsey	Air Gunner	age 27
John Scoular	Air Gunner	age 26

It was continually emphasised by our instructors that it was important that aircrews must work together as a closely knit team (it was no use having a competent pilot if the rear gunner failed to spot a night fighter etc.), and because crews slept in the same hut and ate together it was important that they got on socially.

When I joined this crew I felt happy with the other members, with the exception of the bomb aimer, Smith, who had joined the RAF in peacetime and was contemptuous of those who had joined during the war. After a short while I found the rest of the crew felt the same, so it was decided that the pilot would speak to the commanding officer to ask for a replacement. The C/O agreed without any hesitation, so Smith was replaced by an Australian bomb aimer, 'Hoppy' Hopkinson, who fitted in with us very well.

Before flying with the crew, each member had lectures on the latest scientific equipment available for each particular job. For example, as a navigator, I learned all about the latest radar advances and how to use a visual display unit long before they were generally available. When we finally began flying, the aircraft we trained on was the twin-engined Wellington bomber, which at the start of the war had been the most successful aircraft in Bomber Command, but by 1943 had been replaced as a front line aircraft by the four-engined Lancaster and Halifax bombers. The 'Wimpey' was then used mainly for training.

Our first flying exercises were 'circuits and bumps' – take offs and landings. The crew took their places on board the aircraft (and how little space there was). Alongside the pilot sat the instructor who was in charge of the aircraft for the first flight. He circled the airfield twice and landed. Afterwards he handed the controls to our own pilot and said "You have control." This went on for several days until one day the instructor climbed out of the aircraft and said, "Now on your own…" We all realised that this was our most dangerous flying experience so far. To actually take this huge aircraft off the ground and then land it was no easy matter. Our first take-off was fine, but the landing was very bumpy, however we managed to survive, and went on to take-off and land at night – an even more dangerous business because there were so many airfields in the district and it was possible to get them mixed up. To enable crews to identify their own airfield, a small flashing beacon (known as a pundit) stood in the corner of the field, flashing an identification letter in red.

After our pilot had been passed out as satisfactory flying Wellingtons, flying exercises were given to other members of the crew. For example, there were practice bombing ranges in the Wash, about fifty miles from Desborough. Smoke bombs were loaded on the aircraft and it was the bomb aimer's job to practice bombing these targets, from about ten thousand feet by day and by night. The result of our bombing was telephoned back to Desborough. Our bombing improved with every trip until our bomb aimer achieved an above average marking. Meanwhile on these trips the gunners fired live ammunition at a 'drogue', which is like a wind sock being towed behind another aircraft.

Again as these training exercises were of only short duration the full crew flew each time in order to build up confidence together as well as training the individual member. Having satisfactorily completed this part of the course, it was then the navigator's turn to be examined in detail. This involved about eight cross country trips, four in daylight, and four at night. The navigator was given detailed instructions from which a flight plan was calculated. The instructions included the route to be followed, the height and the speed to fly, the weather forecast and wind. The route was plotted on a navigator's map and most of the other details were recorded on the navigator's log sheet. It was the navigators job to give the pilot instructions so that the aircraft kept to the route. The navigator plotted courses on the chart and kept a detailed log while in the air. All the navigator's paper work was marked by the navigational instructor for every trip. These results proved satisfactory. A typical flight was to fly from Desborough to Hull and then to Carlisle over to Douglas on the Isle of Man, to Oxford then returning to Desborough.

As a crew, we coped very well with these exercises, but there was one occasion, on our return from a night exercise, which could have ended in disaster. One of the problems in this part of the country is the susceptibility to fog, and on this particular occasion, we were the last to take off on the three hour flight, leaving at 11pm and due back at 2am. In the course of the flight, the wireless operator picked up a message about rapidly closing fog. Fog in the air is often only fifty to one hundred feet thick, so when we arrived and flew directly over the airfield the lights stood out clearly. However, when we turned and came in on our landing approach, two or three miles from the runway we could see nothing, because we were looking through two or three miles of fog. We gave up this first attempt at landing and climbed up above the fog. Unlike today, there were no sophisticated aids for landing in fog, and instructions from the control tower simply said 'get down as best you can'. We circled the airfield for about ten minutes while I calculated a course which with luck, would bring us to the end of the runway. Everyone else had landed earlier so we were on our own. We headed down through the fog again after having first shaken hands with each other and offered a silent prayer for our survival. As we turned onto the final approach to the runway, the mental picture I had was of a telegraph boy cycling on his red bike to tell my parents that I had been killed.

As the aircraft went down towards the runway there was a sudden yell from the pilot over the intercom. We were heading for the flare path at a slight angle but there was no possibility of going round again... We bounced twice on the runway, went over onto the grass, just missed the Flight Control Tower and landed up in a ditch! There followed 'cheers' from us all.

The following day Mac Baxter was called into the Flight Commanders Office where he was commended for success- fully getting us down in one piece. We knew some of the airmen who worked in flying control and they said that the general opinion was that we would 'crash' and join two other crews on the course who had crashed on cross country flights, killing everyone.

Not surprisingly, when the bods in the control tower heard our aircraft coming towards them, there was sheer panic as they raced to vacate the tower. However, this incident, which could have ended so tragically, did much to boost confidence in ourselves and our 'Skipper', although we did not talk much about it at the time. Most importantly, there had been no panic amongst our crew. Two nights later we were sent on another cross-country exercise and this time we completed it without any problem.

By now it was at the end of May 1944, and we had completed the course. The Commanding Officer told us, "You are now able, as a crew, to fly the Wellington Bomber, fully loaded to Berlin at night, and return home successfully..." Then, with a big grin on his face he added, "Provided you don't get shot down by flak or by night fighters!"

The next stage of training involved conversion to the four-engined Stirling bomber at Wratting Common near Haverhill, Cambridgeshire.

With my various illnesses I had been at Desborough for about six months and I was glad to be finally leaving. We had 'passed out', but the event went by without much celebration. Looking back it seems quite remarkable that six average young men, who less than a year ago had never been near an aircraft, let alone flown in one, could be trained to this stage. It speaks much for the training methods employed.

We arrived at Wratting common June 1944 and saw the Stirling bomber for the first time. It was a huge four-engined aircraft whose most remarkable feature was the height of the pilot's seat above the ground. It must have been all of twenty feet. The interior of the aircraft was very roomy, in particular the navigator's position, which was big enough to spread a map out fully – very different from the Wellington, which was very cramped. The main drawback was that on operations it had a flying ceiling of about 15,000 feet which made it very vulnerable to the German AA defences. By mid 1944 it had been replaced by the Lancaster and was mainly used thereafter for training and towing gliders.

The main pressure in flying Stirlings was on the pilot, who not only had to deal with four engines but with the problem of landing and take off. Once in the air it was not too difficult to fly. As far as the rest of the crew was concerned, there was not much difference in doing our particular job between a Wellington and Stirling, once we had got used to the instruments.

We were at Wratting Common for about five weeks and during that time our pilot experienced great difficulty in consistently making a good take off and landing. You have to remember that in those days there were no computers to assist in calculating the height from the ground when landing; it was all up to the pilot's judgement. Sometimes we landed smoothly but next time we made an awful bang and bounced down the runway. Ours was not the only pilot who experienced these problems, and it was not unusual for the undercarriage to collapse on landing. In Stirlings, the Bomb Aimer used to help the pilot by holding the throttle open and operating the flaps on take off and landing. After many such exercises we went out one night for further practice. Unfortunately, the Bomb Aimer was sick and after two circuits and landings the instructor called me into the cockpit and said "I'm getting out now and you're on your own." He told me to sit in the second pilot's seat and gave me a few minutes instructions on how to help the pilot. Rarely have I concentrated so hard on picking up instructions, as I realised that failure on my part could kill all of us! Fortunately, we managed to complete the exercises satisfactorily and the instructor passed us out. I was very relieved when the Bomb Aimer returned for the next trip. Having succeeded in getting this massive aircraft off the ground and back again in one piece, we were then put on to the final part of the course which consisted of cross country flying on different exercises.

One of these was a mock night attack on Edinburgh to test their defences against air attack and to give us the impression of what it was like to see searchlights looking for us in the dark, we flew half way out over the North Sea towards Germany and then headed back to the Scottish coast. The exercise was reported as being successful and we thought it invaluable in giving us insight into a real operation.

When we left Desborough we were split up from many of the other crews with whom we had made friends. When we got to Wratting Common we quickly made more friends, our closest friendship was with an Australian pilot called Tug Wilson and his crew. I cannot remember all their names but I can remember Wally the navigator who came from Handsworth in Birmingham and Jimmy the wireless operator who lived at Leicester. Tug was very slightly built, pale-faced and rather quiet. He always seemed to be worried and had similar difficulty flying a Stirling to our pilot. His Navigator, Wally, once said to me that none of them felt that they would survive the course. One night towards the end of the course all the crews had been sent on a cross country trip to Cornwall and out over the Atlantic, returning to Wratting

Common at about 2 am. When we arrived back at base we found that Tug Wilson and his crew were missing. We assumed at the time that they had got lost and had landed elsewhere, but unfortunately we discovered in the morning that Wally's prediction had come true. For some reason their Stirling had crashed near Saffron Walden and there were no survivors. It was very depressing, but we had no time to dwell on it, such things were happening all the time, and in any case we were moved a few days later to the Lancaster finishing school at Feltwell in Norfolk where we were joined by a flight engineer called Ted Rossiter from London, making our crew up to seven.

At Feltwell we were converted from the Stirling to the Lancaster and this proved a quick conversion. The Lancaster was a fine aircraft to fly and much more manoeuvrable than the Stirling. There were no more problems with take-offs and landings.

AIR MINISTRY,
WHITEHALL, S.W.1.

A MESSAGE OF WELCOME

16th February, 1942.

from

THE SECRETARY OF STATE FOR AIR.

You are now an airman and it gives me great pleasure to welcome you into the Royal Air Force.

To have been selected for air crew training is a great distinction. The Royal Air Force demands a high standard of physical fitness and alertness from its flying crews. Relatively few attain that standard, and I congratulate you on passing the stringent tests.

You are, of course, impatient to begin your flying training at once, and the question you ask is "When do I start?" You may rest assured that you will be called up as soon as you are required - and in your turn. While waiting you may carry on with your present job, and equip yourself for your Air Force career by studying subjects which will help you.

The date on which you enter your flying training is decided by various factors - including the requirements of the Service, your age, date of attestation and so on. Once your order on the list is determined you may be sure that you will not be overlooked when your turn comes.

Arrangements will be made to help you in your studies, and you will be told about these in due course. Be sure you make good use of these opportunities. They are important to you.

I feel, however, you will expect me to tell you why it is necessary that you who are so eager should wait at all.

The Royal Air Force is a highly organized Service. In the first line are trained and experienced crews whose stirring deeds and indomitable courage daily provoke the admiration of the world. Behind these men, ready to give them immediate support, are the newly-trained crews fresh from the schools. In your turn you and other accepted candidates stand ready to fill the schools. Without you, time might be lost at a critical moment in filling up the training facilities left vacant by those who have joined the ranks of the first line combatants, and the vital flow of reinforcements would be broken. Vacancies may also be caused by increased training requirements, for the schools are being rapidly expanded. For these reasons we must have a reserve of selected candidates like you on whom to call.

I hope this explanation will help you to understand. The waiting period should not be considered as so much waste of time. There is much you can do. You are exceptionally fit now, or you would not have been chosen. See that you keep fit. Work hard but live temperately. Learn all you can in your spare time about those things you must know if you are to be efficient at your flying job. The more academic knowledge you acquire before you begin your training in the Royal Air Force the easier it will be later on to absorb the specialized Service knowledge.

In wishing you success in the Service of your choice I would like to add this: The Honour of the Royal Air Force is in your hands. Our country's safety and the final overthrow of the powers of evil now arrayed against us depend upon you and your comrades. You will be given the best aircraft and armament that the factories of Britain and America can produce. Equip yourself with knowledge of how to use them.

Good luck!

Archibald Sinclair

SECRETARY OF STATE FOR AIR.

CHAPTER VI

Bomber Command

The Royal Air Force was set up as an independent fighting unit in 1918, at the end of World War I, by combining the Royal Flying Corps and the Royal Naval Air Service.

During the 1920s and 30s there were continuous debates as to the wisdom of having an Air Force operating separately from the Army and Navy. However, when war broke out in 1939 the broad organisation was:-

Fighter Command   to defend ourselves against attack

Coastal Command   to protect convoys and shipping by attacking submarines etc.

Bomber Command   to attack the enemy's homeland by bombing factories, communications etc, thus making it impossible for him to wage war.

After Germany had conquered the whole of Western Europe in June 1940, Bomber Command was the only force able to carry the war to Germany. It was equipped with about 300 twin-engined bombers (e.g. Hampden, Wellington and Whitley) which were capable of carrying 2,000-3,000 lbs of bombs for 1,000 miles at speeds of about 200 mph. They were all armed with machine guns and it was hoped that they could attack targets in daylight. However, these aircraft were no match for the German Fighters (ME109, FW190) and the losses were too heavy to carry on. Sometimes nearly every aircraft sent on a mission was shot down! I knew many lads from Ludlow, just a few years older than me, who simply disappeared in the North Sea.

Soon after the outbreak of war, therefore, Bomber Command was forced to attack Germany at night. Most nights BBC Radio reported from the Air Ministry that bombers had attacked targets in Germany and I remember how much this raised civilian morale with the thought that the Germans were 'receiving some of their own medicine'.

In September 1940 Winston Churchill, then British Prime Minister said:

> *"The fighters are our salvation but the bombers alone provide the means of victory. We must therefore develop the power to carry on ever increasing volume of explosives to Germany so as to pulverise the entire industry and scientific structure on which the war effort and economic life of the enemy depend, while holding him at arms length from our island."*

Unknown to the general population, the Government was unhappy at the huge sums being poured into Bomber Command with apparently poor results. A special report prepared in 1942 showed that very few Bombers reached their target and that their effect was negligible.

However, in June 1941, Hitler attacked Russia which was in great danger of defeat within a few months and was only saved by the Russian winter. We all realised at the time that if Russia was defeated we in Britain stood no chance of defeating Germany, and the only practical way of helping Russia was by increasing our bombing of Germany so that they would have to use vital men and supplies to defend themselves.

With this in mind, steps were taken in 1942 to increase the size of Bomber Command by manufacturing 4-engined heavy bombers with greater range, bomb load and armour. Airfields were built all over East Anglia, Lincolnshire and Yorkshire (by 1944 there were about 100 Bomber Command Bases). Accuracy of the bombing was improved by introducing scientific aids to Air Navigation and Bombing and marking targets with coloured flares.

All these measures had a very significant effect, as about 2,000,000 German servicemen were employed in home defence (instead of fighting in Russia).

The intensity of the Bomber Command Offensive between 1942 and the end of the war in 1945 was matched by the brilliant defence of the German Luftwaffe, which meant very heavy losses on both sides. These casualties became even larger when the American 8th Air Force joined the campaign with fighter-escorted daylight bombing of Germany in 1943, 1944 and 1945. At the end of the war, RAF Bomber Command had about 1,600 four-engined aircraft (mainly Lancasters) capable of dropping 5-6 tons of bombs each. In the battles over Germany 47,000 RAF aircrew were killed and about 4,000 were interned, one in two men taking part. Something over 7,000 Lancasters alone were shot down.

You can see that it needed lots of luck as well as skill for a bomber crew to survive a 'tour of duty' (30 operations). It was into this background that our crew came into Bomber command in July 1944.

After about two weeks we were 'passed out' as a crew able to be posted to a squadron and fit for operational flying. We were transported by lorry to 622 Squadron at Mildenhall, Suffolk. On the lorry with us was another crew who had also 'passed out' and were being posted to 15 Squadron, also based at Mildenhall. On the fifteen mile journey from Feltwell we were laughing and joking with each other about our chances of survival. A week later, we heard that they had been shot down on their first flight over Germany with no survivors. This came as no surprise to us as we knew only too well that Bomber Command casualties were high.

Reading this story so far you could be forgiven for thinking that we were all serious young men devoted to flying. In fact, for much of the time we were grounded because of bad weather, unserviceable aircraft, or illness. We amused ourselves usually by going to the camp cinema, if there was one, or taking the free RAF bus to the nearest town. For example, the airfield at Desborough was very isolated so a bus was provided to take us to Kettering. Here we used to go as a crew into the local pubs, especially those with a piano, where we could have a good 'sing-song'.

When I joined the RAF I did not smoke at all and only rarely had the odd half pint of bitter. On joining the crew at Desborough I found that they were drinking four or five pints a night and smoking about forty cigarettes per day, as these were very cheap, and often sent as presents from home. After a few weeks of going out with them, I found I could also drink and smoke like them without having a hangover. Generally speaking, I found the relationship between local people and servicemen in the pub was good. One night, however, there was an incident in Kettering that could have been nasty. An argument developed in the corner of the pub between an RAF man and some locals. Normally, we would have avoided getting involved, but because we'd had a few drinks we felt we should join in on the side of the RAF man. Quite a few other RAF boys did the same. Quite understandingly, the Landlord of the pub became alarmed and called the police, who threw everyone out into the street where the argument continued and the situation became ugly. Suddenly, one of the policeman shouted "Come on lads – it's Hitler we're fighting and it's Berlin we want!" His comment broke the tension and soon the RAF, the locals and the police were singing patriotic songs together in the middle of Kettering. Eventually, everyone dispersed peacefully.

To return to my main story... Mildenhall was one of the largest RAF stations in the country. It was a permanent airfield. The buildings were constructed of brick and in addition to offices and briefing rooms there were many married quarters. The whole base was linked by properly constructed tarmac roads. It was a very comfortable camp to be at and each crew was allotted to a small house. Mildenhall was the place from which the England/Australia Air race started in 1934. In the 1950s it was leased to the American airforce and became the main transport base between Britain and America. On returning for a reunion in 1982 the base was like a small piece of America and dollars were the only currency acceptable.

Before reaching Mildenhall I had already been on four other airfields. Each one had caused a tingle of excitement, but then we knew that our flying would be over friendly home territory. Mildenhall was quite different. There were about 40 Lancasters (20 to each squadron) scattered at dispersal round the airfield. It was quite normal to see 'bombing up trolleys' travelling from the bomb dumps to the Lancasters, loaded with high explosives and incendiaries. These were handled by trained armourers who installed the bombs into the aircraft bomb racks and loaded the ammunition belts which fed the machine guns in the turrets. There were also many big petrol 'bowsers' filling the aircraft with aviation spirit. All this activity created an atmosphere of tension, as plans for attack on the enemy were developed.

After a few days of settling in we were ordered to report to the Wing Commander's office. Here we were met by the Wing Commander himself, Ian Swales who was accompanied by the head of each section of the aircrew e.g. the chief Navigation Officer, the chief Bomb Aimer etc. Ian Swales was a tall slim man of about 28, who had joined the RAF as a boy entrant in the mid-1930s. He qualified as a pilot early in the war, and had completed we understood, two tours of operations for which he was decorated DSO, DFC, DSM. He had blonde hair and a big handle-bar moustache, and to everyone he was affectionately known as 'Blondie'. Although officially he and his senior officer should not have flown on operations because of the heavy loss that would have been sustained if they were shot down, nevertheless, on some of the most difficult targets they would fly in other aircraft with us. He was very quietly spoken and talked to us for about ten minutes. He said we would be at Mildenhall until we had completed thirty operations over Germany or German occupied Europe. If we completed these operations we would get six months rest from flying. While at Mildenhall we were allowed one week's leave after three weeks flying. He advised us not to count the operations we were doing, to forget the future, and concentrate 100 per cent on every flight.

"There is no such thing as an easy target," he said ominously, adding that it was not unusual to find German aircraft flying over Suffolk, looking for unsuspecting bombers to shoot down.

We listened attentively to his remarks, asked one or two questions as to when we would start flying and were told that the first step would be for our 'skipper' Mac Baxter to act as second pilot to an experienced crew on an operation to a major German target. If he came back, he would then take us over, and we would fly as a crew.

After this meeting we were allowed a few days to familiarise ourselves with the airbase, for example, I located the Navigators' room where all the navigators in the squadron reported each day whether flying or not. We sat around, smoked and chatted about the state of the war, and incidents about flying on operations. The chief Navigation Officer was always present, he was a small Canadian from Winnipeg and had completed a 'tour' of 30 operations. After every operational flight each navigator handed in his log and navigational chart to the Navigational Officer, who would check them in detail, and then discuss them with the Navigator concerned, giving advice on the ways in which the performance could be improved. He frequently used to have a general discussion amongst all of us and gave out some very useful tips. I remember particularly, him telling us how to keep track of the aircraft position after it had bombed the target. Usually, when the bombs have been dropped the bomb aimer would yell "bombs gone, bomb doors closed, lets get the hell out of here!" The pilot always had the Navigator's calculated course to leave the target but was usually driven off course by heavy anti-aircraft fire and searchlights. As the aircraft twisted and turned, you can imagine how difficult it was for the navigator to keep track of its position, but by using one of the Canadian Navigation Officer's tips, the navigator still managed to retain control.

When you opened the door of the navigation room, immediately opposite on the wall was pinned a big picture of Bomber Command Commander-in-Chief, a very tough and stern looking Sir Arthur Harris. The words under the picture said quite simply:

'WHEN HE SAYS YOU GO, YOU GO!'

How true these words were, because if you failed to destroy the target to his satisfaction one night, he would send you back a second night, or third, until he was satisfied. This was measured from the reconnaissance photographs taken after each raid, and supported by pictures taken from every aircraft automatically after the heavy bombs were dropped.

This was partly to see the effect on the target, but also to ensure that reluctant crews did not simply dump their bombs into the North Sea. Unless there was a valid picture, the raid did not count towards one's tour of duty.

The other important room all Aircrew, and particularly Navigators, were encouraged to visit, was the Intelligence room. Here the Intelligence Officer laid out all the latest intelligence information about Germany and occupied Europe; this included the location of the anti-aircraft guns, searchlight batteries, fighter airfields etc.

The other members of the crew had their own meeting rooms e.g. Pilots, Bomb Aimers, and so on. When we all came together as a crew, we had pretty good knowledge of the workings of the air base and of Germany. Every day a battle order was posted on the main noticeboard, this gave details of every crew who was to stand by for flying on that day/ night. Our first flight from Mildenhall, was a short trip to familiarise ourselves with the local area, picking out many landmarks, for example, Ely Cathedral.

For some unexplained reason I had always been keen to experience flying in the rear gunner turret. I mentioned this to Frank Ramsay our Rear Gunner who, before I could change my mind asked Mac Baxter if I could try this, amidst grins from the other members of the crew. I climbed into the rear turret. What a terrible feeling of isolation it gave me as the pilot threw the aircraft round the sky. After about 15 minutes of this I shouted over the intercom, "I've had enough!" and amidst cheers, I climbed out of the turret, looking as white as a sheet and feeling thoroughly airsick. After this experience

A/C No.	LETTER	CPT & 2ND PLT.	NAV & W/
HA.228	A.	F/O Benson.	F/Sgt. W / F/S Mone
NF.939	B.	F/O Jones	W.O. Rob / W.O. Mor
HK.621	C.	W.O. Hanson.	Sgt. Hol / F/S Drum
PK.677.	D.	F/O Phillips	Sgt. Low / Sgt. Burt
M.577	E.	F/S Francis	Sgt. Stog / Sgt. Kel
DI.235	G.	F/O Baxter	Sgt. Par / Sgt. Bro
NN.709	H.	F/O Armitstead / F/O Elsmon	F/S Brow / Sgt. Ha
LL.885	J.	F/O Peck	F/S Bard / F/O Garg
NF.964	L.	F/S Richards	F/S Kidd / Sgt. Doy
PD.332.	N.	F/O Bonner.	F/S Brod / F/S Vaug
DI.283	O.	F/Lt. Orton	F/O Simp / Sgt. Col
PB.164	P	F/S Campbell	Sgt. Salt / F/S Joz
HK.614	R.	F/O Cox	F/O Taylo / F/S Shno
LL.803	S.	F/Lt. Dean / F/Lt. Chas	F/C Mead / Sgt. Mac
NF.615	U.	F/O Nicholls	F/S Pond / Sgt. Gre
DI.282	V.	F/O Richards	F/O Inbo / Sgt. Hurt
HK.616	W.	F/O Woods	F/S Groet / Sgt. John
HK.617	Y	F/O Bussey.	F/O Simps / Sgt. May
HK615	Z	F/S Clarke	F/C Pantl / F/S Willi

Officer i/c Flying Rations. :) W/C Benson.(Rations obtainable f
F/C Benson's Crew to stand by for Radar.

PILOT.	A/B & W.U.GUNR.	M.GUNR. & F/ENGINER.
	F/S Dilley	Sgt. Woolloff.
	Sgt. Dutch	Sgt. Boulton.
	F/ Pidley	Sgt. Smith.
	Sgt. Rogers	Sgt. Hills.
	F/S Stewart	Sgt. Crawford.
	Sgt. Abbott F/S Dut.	Sgt. Armstrong.
	Sgt. Smart	Sgt. York.
	Sgt. Morgan	Sgt. Barber.
	Sgt. Traylen	Sgt. Purten.
	Sgt. Baxter	Sgt. Soanos.
	F/S Hopkinson	Sgt. Ernsoy.
	Sgt. Scouller	Sgt. Rositer.
	Sgt. Daniels	Sgt. Borro.
	Sgt. Koylock	Sgt. Pock.
	P/O Daws	Sgt. Rudney.
	Sgt. Ramsey	Sgt. Dowyer.
	F/O Mildren	Sgt. Michelson.
	Sgt. Pupps	Sgt. Martin.
	F/O Ward	F/S Horan.
	F/S Lothian	Sgt. Beacham.
	F/O Humphreys	W.O Prince.
	Sgt. Strong	Sgt. Davis.
	F/S Shenley	Sgt. Hickling.
	Sgt. Fellows	Sgt. Hill.
	F/O Titchenor	Sgt. Gilroy.
	Sgt. Matthews	Sgt. Huynce.
	F/S Bullock	Sgt. Brown.
	Sgt. Harland	Sgt. Willicombe.
	F/S Smith	Sgt. Smith.
	Sgt. Bond	Sgt. Lawson.
	P/O Carter	Sgt. Campbell.
	Sgt. Drylcy	Sgt. Burnard.
	Sgt. Taylor W.O.	Sgt. Gentley.
	Sgt. Henderson	Sgt. Spency.
	F/S Dalton F/S McRae	Sgt. O'Conner.
	Sgt. Potter	Sgt. Hand.
	F/S Chaplin	Sgt. Bryson.
	Sgt. Bryant	Sgt. Booth.

Discip Office Key in Guardroom.)

) I.C.K. Swales DSO DFC DFM
 Wing Commander, Commanding No. 622 Squadron.

I always had the greatest respect for rear gunners who did such an essential job, scouring the sky for enemy fighters.

This reminds me of a rather sad story. When I was at Mildenhall, I used to travel from Birmingham by train from New Street to Bletchley Junction, from where I would catch the train to Cambridge. At that time a Rear Gunner from another crew who lived at Oldbury near Birmingham travelled with me. His name was Percy Withers. There was a famous American film star at the time called Jane Withers, so we naturally nick-named him 'Jane' – he didn't seem to mind. On returning from leave, I met him and his father on New Street Station. He was about 19 and his father about 40. His father travelled with us to Bletchley, where we stood for half an hour, waiting for our connection to Cambridge. His father wished us well and said he looked forward to seeing us again soon. That was the last time he ever saw his son, who was killed in a battle with a night fighter over Kiel. He was the only casualty amongst his crew. Every time I hear mention of the words 'Rear Gunner' my mind flashes back to this incident and to Percy Withers and his dad.

We realised that once we had done these familiarisation flights around Mildenhall it would not be long before we became involved in flying on operations. In the short time we had been at Mildenhall we became aware of the roar of aircraft engines as Lancasters took off and landed. We heard from crews who had been there a few weeks that most of the targets were German cities. Several aircraft were missing, having been shot down. Some returned badly damaged. We were told of one incident, where the Pilot of a Lancaster had been badly injured in a raid on the German Naval Base of Kiel. He was awarded the DSO immediately, because of bravery in getting the aircraft back.

About the middle of August our pilot Mac Baxter appeared on the Battle Order as a second pilot to a crew that had already done fifteen operations. This was a moment we had all been dreading, because if he was shot down on this operation we would be left without a pilot and skipper. This would have been a severe blow to us, having worked together as a crew for the previous four months. We all said cheerio to him as he made his way the Briefing Room in the early evening. Details of any operation were TOP SECRET to everyone except those taking part and the top Commanders, so we had no idea where he was going. However, we knew it was a German target because we had heard through the grapevine that the bomb load consisted of a 4,000 lb blast bomb (known as a 'cookie') and also incendiaries. The petrol for this trip was about 2,000 gallons, so we deduced it was a deep penetration into Germany. We heard the squadron aircraft take off at about 9 pm and we sat down to pass the time, smoking, drinking and playing cards.

At about 2.30 am we heard the first aircraft arrive back, followed quickly by a succession of other aircraft. We began to feel even more on edge than usual as the minutes ticked away. After about an hour we began to hear footsteps in the road as crews returned to their billets after being de-briefed whilst having an early breakfast. At last we heard footsteps coming our way. They stopped outside the door. Someone gave three loud bangs and a broad Scots voice shouted,

"Open this bloody door!" We gave a cheer, opened the door, slapped him on the back and poured him a pint of beer. Naturally, we could hardly wait to hear how he had got on. He told us that the target had been some aircraft factories in 'Brunswick' – about seventy miles west of Berlin. We knew from previous accounts of raids that this was heavily defended, and Mac confirmed there was heavy anti-aircraft fire and he had seen several Lancasters shot down by fighters.

He had survived... but we knew that we were in for a very tough time over the following months.

About this time, we were given a short course on how to get into a dingy if the aircraft should come down into the sea, and also how to abandon the aircraft by parachute. When we started flying we were taught these things at an early stage, but now were near to flying in combat it was important for us to have a refresher course.

The duty of every member of the armed forces is to avoid capture, or if captured to make every effort to escape and return to his base by any means available. In occupied Europe, for example, the resistance movement had organised transport communications from Holland, Belgium and France and across the Pyrenees through to Spain (which was neutral). The British Embassy would organise transport through to Gibraltar from where the airman could be flown back to England. Many shot down airmen completed this journey successfully. Some were caught, and sent to prisoner of war camps, whilst their resistance helpers were shot.

Any crew shot down over Germany itself had a much more difficult task to avoid capture as there was no resistance movement to assist them. In order to help them avoid capture, aircrews were issued with escape equipment, which was carried on every flight. I cannot remember all the things we carried, but here are some of them:

Safety razor	Collar stud compass
Horlicks tablets	Whistle
Small bars of chocolate	Maps on silk handkerchiefs
First aid dressing	Dutch & French banknotes
Fishing line & bait	Knife

This equipment proved invaluable according to airmen who had been forced to bale out. Fortunately for my crew, although we had many near escapes, as you will read in the following pages, we did not have to jump. However, the following experience was related to me after the war by a close friend, Michael Connolly. Michael, born in 1922, was one year older than me. He qualified as a Navigator in South Africa and was eventually posted to a Bomber Command Squadron in Yorkshire, flying Halifaxes. At the end of 1943 and the beginning of 1944 Bomber Command was involved in a succession of heavy raids over the German capital, Berlin. Berlin was one of the most heavily defended cities in the world, especially by anti aircraft guns and searchlights. There were heavy losses. On one such raid Michael's aircraft was on its final run towards the target when there was an enormous explosion as an AA shell burst alongside. The aircraft immediately went out of control and the skipper gave the command to 'bale out'. Michael said he could barely remember where he had put his parachute, but after a few seconds fumbling in the darkness, he managed to find it and quickly put it on. He made his way to the escape hatch where three others were waiting their turn to jump. Although it seemed like an eternity to Michael, it could have only been about two minutes since the explosion until he was floating at the end of the parachute in the Berlin night sky. Shortly after they had jumped, the aircraft blew up, scattering flaming pieces of aircraft everywhere. Michael learned afterwards, that one of these pieces had landed on top of his pilot's parachute. In spite of desperate efforts to shake it off, the flaming wreckage burned an ever increasing hole in his parachute, with the result that the speed of descent became faster and faster. Eventually, the pilot crashed through the roof of a farmhouse, past the foot of the bed in which the farmer and his wife were sleeping and came to rest in the lounge. He was, of course, very badly injured, with broken legs and arms, but astonishingly, had survived.

In the meantime, Michael had successfully landed in a Berlin suburb, he released his parachute and hid it behind a garden wall. Although he apparently had no physical injuries, he was badly shocked and disoriented. He heard the last of the RAF bombers returning to England and felt a wave of severe depression. Only a few hours earlier he had been having a drink at the airfield in Yorkshire, now he was alone in the middle of a hostile country. He cut off the top of his flying boots, which left him wearing shoes and tried to look like a civilian. He wandered around and a postman even said 'good morning' to him. However, he had no realistic chance of avoiding capture, and eventually was picked up by a policeman and taken to a police station nearby where there were other aircrew who had been shot down. They had a great fear of being attacked by German civilians taking revenge for attacks on their city, however, about mid-morning they were bundled onto lorries and driven through Berlin to the Gestapo headquarters at Frankfurt-on-Maine. While they were travelling through Berlin the tarpaulin covers blew open several times and they could see the devastation caused by the British and American air attacks. Many people seemed to be living in caves made out of the rubble.

At Frankfurt-on-Maine they were questioned individually by the police, who already had a surprising amount of knowledge about the RAF. Michael gave them the minimum of information: his number, rank and name and when they realised he had nothing much to tell them he was sent to a prisoner of war camp in Poland – Stalag Luft III. Here he met the Bomb Aimer of his crew and they found out that five out of the seven crew had survived.

In the winter of 1944-1945 the Russian Army was advancing into Poland towards Germany. The Germans decided to evacuate the prisoners westwards towards Western Germany. The prisoners were formed into columns and force-marched up to twenty miles a day in freezing conditions, harrassed by German guards. Overnight they sought cover where they could. Prisoners who were too ill to march were shot by the guards on the spot. The columns of prisoners, after several months, reached an area near Bremen which had been captured by the British Army. The German guards abandoned their prisoners, who were eventually picked up by the British Army and flown back to England.

After the war, owing to the conditions he endured in Germany, Michael suffered from severe digestion problems. He underwent many operations to correct the damage but eventually died at the early age of sixty. He was a very kind man with a most considerate nature. With my experience of flying we were able to talk on equal terms, and having heard his story I was more grateful than ever that I had not been shot down.

The overall object of RAF Bomber Command was laid down by the British War Cabinet. They would issue orders in general terms for example: destroy the German Aircraft Industry or Oil Plants. Within these objectives Bomber Command Headquarters at High Wycombe would decide which cities and factories were to be attacked. These decisions were taken every day. The necessary instructions included routes to be taken, timings, and the target, were sent to group Headquarters, and then to the individual squadron who were responsible for carrying out the attack.

On 13th August 1944 our names appeared on the Battle Order for the first time. The Battle Order was a list of crews to be ready for the next attack, and the aircraft allocated to them. While every raid was different in location of the target, nevertheless in principle, the pre-flight preparation and post flight interrogation were very similar. Each member of the crew reported to his own section to be briefed in detail about his own job. This took place several hours before take off. As far as I was concerned, as Navigator there was always a considerable amount of work to be done. When all the Navigators on the Battle Order turned up at the Navigators Room we were given all the details required to draw up plans for the raid. Once again I cannot guarantee to have remembered everything but the main information is a follows:

1. Latitude and Longitude of the target
2. Routes to be taken to the target and the return home
3. The height and speed to be flown on the route
4. The times to be over the turning point and over the target
5. The weather forecast including the wind direction and strength over the whole route
6. Any other specific orders that were given, for example to keep a watch for rocket launching sights and flying bomb sites

Using the above information and a calculator, the navigator prepared a flight plan for the raid and set down all the details on his log sheet. He also obtained a special chart which covered the area involved, and drew on the chart the route and all the known details of the German defences to be avoided. Having checked these calculations amongst the navigators, we were then joined by the other members of the crew. Shortly afterwards, we had a meal in the canteen, got dressed into our flying kit and went along to the main briefing room, where all the crews were assembled. Permanently fixed to the one wall was a large map of the UK, Germany and occupied Europe. On the map would appear the route and target for tonight's particular raid. We all sat down talking. Suddenly, the noise stopped as the Group Captain entered the room, and we all stood to attention. Having told us to be seated, he gave a general briefing on the raid, the reason why it was to be carried out, how the target would be marked by flares, and any other information he thought would be useful.

Having answered any questions, he was followed by the Chief Intelligence Officer and finally by the Met man, who gave the weather forecast for the trip. He was always subject to good natured 'booing' because on many an occasion the forecast would be for cloud cover over the target only for crews to find a bright starlit sky when they got there. This was very bad news, because such conditions would result in the German fighters shooting down many of the attacking bombers. In spite of this, however, the Met men did a very good job in extremely difficult circumstances, and the 'booing' had much to do with relieving the tension which was building up amongst the aircrews.

Briefing over, we went to the parachute room, put on a 'MaeWest' life jacket and parachute harness and collected our parachute. We then waited outside for transport to the aircraft which were standing on dispersal pans around the airfield. On many raids we flew in 'G' for George, so when the lorry driver shouted out "Who's for George?" we would all jump out and sit on the grass by the aircraft. Sometimes we joked, but frequently we just sat and smoked cigarettes thinking our own thoughts and wondering whether in a few hours we would still be alive. Even at this late stage raids could be cancelled, so we waited for the signal from the Control Tower: either a green flare would be fired into the air, which meant that the 'op' was going ahead, or a red one if it was cancelled.

Generally speaking, the green cartridge was fired, and shortly after this the Group Captain in charge of the base would drive around in a van to every aircraft, asking if there were any problems and wishing everyone 'good luck'. We would then begin to climb aboard, having first looked under the open bomb doors to see the bomb load, which usually consisted of a 4,000 lb 'cookie' surrounded by incendiary bombs, and other high explosives, making about five tons in all. Whatever the rights and wrongs of war, I always felt a certain amount of sympathy for the people on whom these bombs were to be dropped. But we, like the Germans, had a job to do.

Once aboard the aircraft, we took up our various positions, the bomb doors were closed, and the skipper with the help of the ground crew, and the huge starting battery, started up the engines. We then carried out a detailed check of the parts for which each of us was responsible. As a Navigator, I checked all the radar navigational equipment and the compasses. When this had all been completed, each reported back to the skipper, who in the meantime, with the Flight Engineer had been checking the engines, fuel capacity, etc. Once we were satisfied that the aircraft was OK, a 'Form 700' was signed by the skipper and passed to the Ground Staff. We were now ready to take off, and this was reported to the Control Tower, who, in due course would give instruc-

SQUADRON................. A/C NUMBER AND LETTER............. F. .... CAPTA[IN]

FORECAST W/Vs AND AIR TEMPS.

TAGE	FROM TO	.000 FT		.000 FT		.000 FT		.000 FT		.000 FT	
		From (T)	Speed	From (T)	Speed	From (T)	Speed	From (T)	Speed	From (T)	Speed
		TEMP °C		TEMP °C		TEMP °C		TEMP °C		TEMP °C	

TIME	RQD TRACK (T)	W/V USED AND COMPUTED DRIFT	Course (T)	VARN	Course (M)	Compass Corrn. for Devn.	Course (C)	FROM:—
.02	043	215/25	044	10W	054			BASE
18	048	215/25	050	9W	059	—		CROMER
46	079	215/25	084	8W	090			
12	079	220/30	084	8W	090			
21	148	225/32	157	7W	164			
40	148	230/35	157	7W	164			
45½	102	240/30	107	6W	113			
3.58	086	240/30	087	6W	093			
086	057	240/30	088	6W	094			
09¾	342	230/38	338	6W	344			
13½	342	224/27	336	6W	332			
19½	289	215/22	285	6W	291			
23½	289	210/18	287½	7W	291			
	235	215/22	233	8W	241			
	223	215/25	224	9W	231			

Navigator's Log entries for a raid on Bremen

=|S BAXTER | NAVIGATOR Sgt PARSONS | DATE 19. 2. 44

POSITION	SUN		MOON		TWILIGHT		FOR
	RISES	SETS	RISES	SETS	A.M.	P.M.	441
BREMEN 1st German operation				1818 44			

CH......... fast slow AT......... GMT. ON...../...../... GD. RATE......... secs./hr. gaining losing

DERS ʃo = ... ⅟ft 0010 - 0012. T.O. 21.20 S/c 22.02
...s 30°6 130 ...x 27 ⅖°/o C AFet 21.10. [2359 Ha
Haven. ...nes G. T's 02.46. 29% s/c
...feu 2000/15 0500 climb 155 to 16,500 ... 150 to 20000
...t 160 to 10m. from tgt.

ROUTE TO:—	R.A.S.	HEIGHT & AIR TEMP.	T.A.S.	D.R. G/S	DIST. TO RUN	D.R. TIME	E.T.A
—A CROMER	175	12/+14	179	202	55	16.	22.18
—B 53.50 0800	175	12/+14	179	202	95	28	22.46
—C 54.05 0500	175	12/+14	179	198	85	26	23.12
—D 54.10 05.45	155	10/+5	183	208	32	9	23.21
—E E.coast	150	18/-10	202	190	61	19.	23.40
—F 53.12 0648	160	20/-15	223	218	20	5½	23.45
—G 53.03 0800	160	20/-15	223	246	52	12½	23.58
—A 53.05 0847	180	20/-15	250	278	34	8	0006
—H 53.06 09.10	180	20/-15	250	278	16	34	0094
—I DR.	240	16/-6	320	330	22	4½	0015
—J 53.42 08.50	180	12/0	219	230	23	6	0019
—K E.coast	240	7/+8	279	270	18	4	0033
—L 54.30 0500	180	2/+14	188	182	148	49.	01.12
—A CROMER.	180	2/+14	188	172	187	65	02.17
BASE	80.	2/+14	188	171	55	19.	02.36
—							
—							

tions to taxi the aircraft from the dispersal point onto the perimeter track and make our way to the runway for take off.

Once I had checked the navigational equipment and laid out the various maps on the table, there was nothing more for me to do until we were airborne, so I used to either stand by the pilot, or stand in the astrodome, to see what was happening on the airfield. This was an awe inspiring sight, as there was a queue of 25 or so Lancasters, slowly making their way for take off. On the edge of the runway at the take off point, there was a small black and white chequered caravan, manned by WAAFs and airmen from flying control. As the aircraft stood with roaring engines at the end of the runway, a signal from the caravan waved 'Good Luck', and with its massive bomb load, the Lancaster would rumble down the runway, until it reached a hundred and ten miles per hour when it slowly became airborne.

This was always one of the most tense moments of any flight, as there were plenty of examples of aircraft crashing on take off with disastrous results as the bomb loads blew up. We had one very precarious moment when the Flight Engineer raised the flaps before being ordered to do so by the pilot. The aircraft, which at that stage was only a few hundred feet off the ground, sank downwards, and it took a considerable effort, to keep it airborne. We all thought the end had come and the Flight Engineer was vigorously sworn at. He never made the same mistake again!

Once airborne, I, as Navigator, switched on the small lamp in my compartment and drew the curtains around me without any light escaping. It was my job to instruct the Pilot of the compass courses to fly, the speed, and height, and to tell all the crew over the intercom where we were, and what to look out for. They in turn, would pass observations back to me. In this way, as a team effort, we kept the aircraft in the right position, because whereas the German Airforce would send bombers over England all night in small waves, Bomber Command would send hundreds of aircraft over a target, completing the raid in half an hour, with the purpose of completely swamping the German defences, and so reducing our losses.

As we circled East Anglia, gaining height as darkness fell I would have a quick look out of the astrodome and see dozens of aircraft from other airfields joining us. At a predetermined time we all headed for the Continent and the target to be attacked. Once darkness had fallen, we saw no other aircraft, but we knew we were surrounded by them, and occasionally we started to bump around as we got caught in the slipstream of another aircraft.

When I said to the pilot that the target was coming up ahead, he would say, "I can see it. Look at all the bloody flak coming up!" He would then tell the Bomb Aimer to take over. On the way over the Continent the crew would report the build up of German defences as their guns and night fighters attacked the 'bomber stream'. All this activity was recorded by me in the log.

In normal life, time slips by unnoticed, but there were occasions in the lives of bomber crews when a few seconds or minutes could seem like eternity. Time always seemed to slow down on final approach, when the Bomb Aimer took control of the aircraft. 'Hoppy', our Bomb Aimer would say, "OK Skipper, I can see it. Left a bit... Right a bit... Keep her steady... Bomb doors open... Steady, steady... Bombs gone! Lets get the hell out of here!'

The skipper would push the nose down, and at about 300mph dive out of the area. I would then take over again and give compass courses to fly back to our base at Mildenhall. Thankfully, we would arrive home safely and join the circuit for instructions from the Control Tower to land. Landing, was always another tense moment, because there was always the danger that the aircraft could have been damaged in some way that we couldn't see. (Fortunately, in our case, this didn't ever occur.)

We would then be taken back to a debriefing room where every crew was given a detailed interview by Intelligence Officers. At this stage, we were given a welcome tot of rum. At the end of the interview we were finally dismissed and went to the canteen for what was, in those days of rationing, the fantastic luxury of a fried bacon and egg breakfast and then to bed.

Between 14th August and 4th December 1944 we flew 31 operations, of which 24 were against German targets. Taking into account that those dates included three weeks leave, on average we flew one operation every three days – quite a schedule! A few of these operations were 'a piece of cake' (RAF slang for 'no problem'). Other operations were just the opposite, and we were lucky to survive them. When we were interviewed by the Wing Commander he had said, "If possible we like to break new crews in gently." In our case, he was as good as his word, because our first attack was a three and a half hour return flight to St. Trond, a big German night fighter base, east of Brussels. This was a daylight raid, by several hundred Lancasters, heavily supported by British fighters, who kept the Luftwaffe away from the bombers. What a strange feeling as we left the English coast behind, and for the first time crossed the enemy coast of Belgium. It was equally weird to fly through the horrible black puffs of smoke left by bursting anti-aircraft shells ('flak' – as it was called). When an AA shell burst it would send hundreds of small pieces of jagged metal flying around the sky. Just one of these pieces hitting a vital part could bring an aircraft down.

It was with a sigh of relief that we landed back at Mildenhall undamaged. For the reminder of August, we were not so lucky with our targets. We bombed German targets at night three times, each one more difficult and dangerous than the one before.

We started by bombing the docks at Bremen, followed by an attack on the Opel car factory at Frankfurt, where we were told they were making tanks, and finally an attack on the docks at Stettin on the Baltic coast, north east of Berlin. The raid on Stettin filled me with more apprehension than any of the other 30 missions we flew. By August 1944, the German army on the Eastern front had been driven by the Russian army into Poland and towards Germany itself. To supply its eastern army, Germany was sending considerable supplies from the Baltic port of Stettin and Bomber Command was urged by the Russians to bomb it. The most direct route from England to Stettin, was across heavily defended North West

DAILY EXPR

No. 13,811   Black-out 9.6 pm to 6.52 am   WEDNESDAY SEPTEMBER 6 1944   Moon ris

Bomber fleets roar into the Battle for the Ports as the armies mass on the German frontier

1,000 TON RAID HITS HAVRE

Blitz on Brest : Heavy fighting for Boulogne

CONCENTRATED might of the Allied air fleets was unleashed for the final battles of Havre, the Channel ports and the Siegfried Line yesterday as Allied armies massed on the German frontiers for the grand assault on the Reich.

After the Germans in Havre had been given one last chance to surrender and had turned it down, more than a thousand tons of bombs were dropped before nightfall by R.A.F. Lancasters on positions round the fortress town.

The bombers went over wave after wave for two hours. Other Lancasters bombed Brest.

Flying Fortresses went to the Rhineland and Brest in force. Behind the Siegfried Line the key supply towns of Karlsruhe and Ludwigsaven were bombed by more than 500 of the

---

The Daily Express reports
the Le Havre raid.

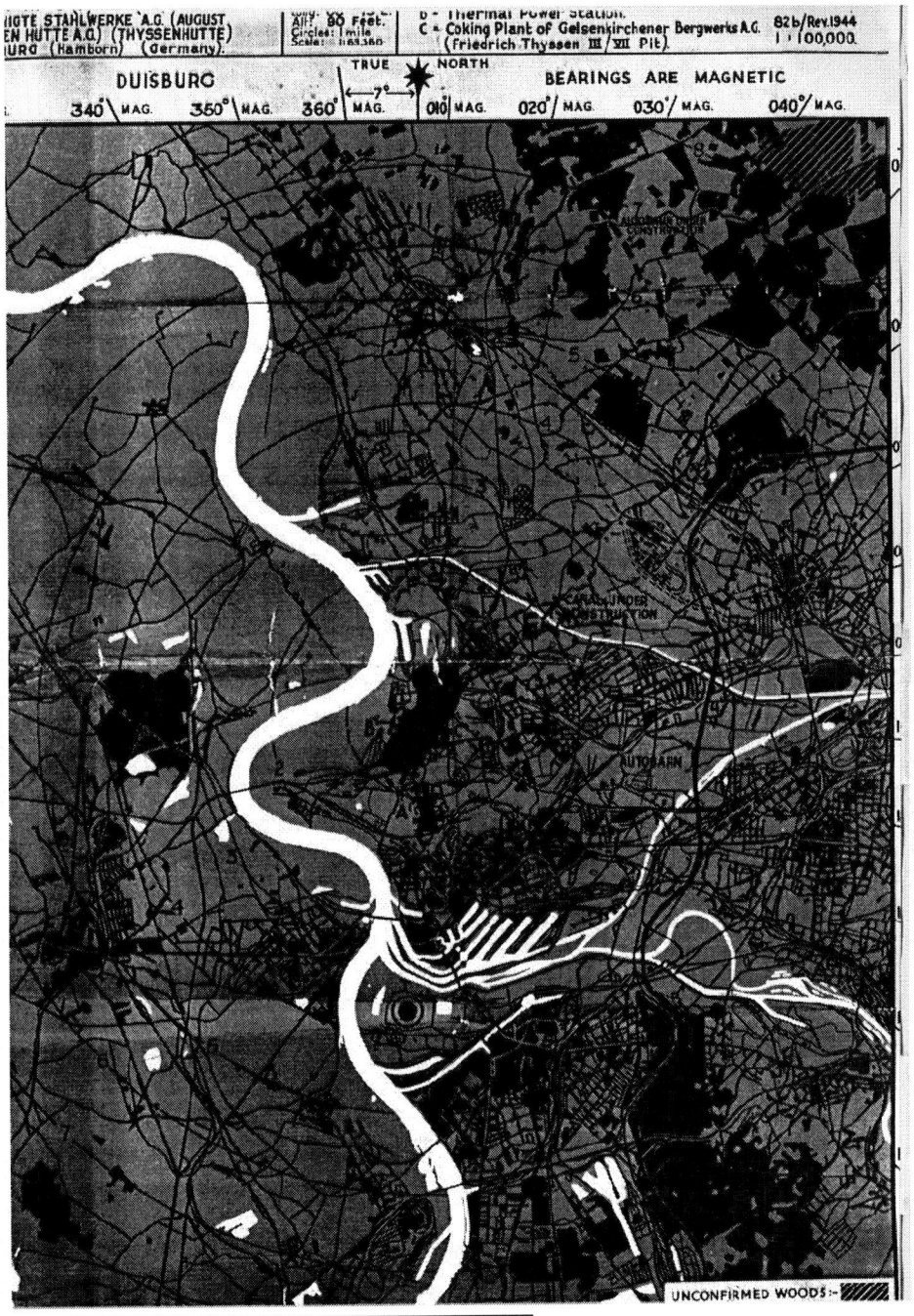

*A Bomb-Aimer's map (this one is of Duisburg)
depicting a night-time view of the target.*

Germany, which would have caused very heavy losses. This was the explanation given for the very long route we were given at the Navigational briefing. We were ordered to leave Mildenhall at 8pm, to cross the English coast at Cromer and then head towards the North West coast of Denmark. Having crossed Denmark, the route headed South East over Sweden, even though it was a neutral country. Our next turning point was to be Bornholm, a Danish Island off the Southern coast of Sweden. From here we headed over the Baltic Sea towards Berlin, as though we were going to attack it. This was an attempt to deceive the German defences, because we suddenly turned away from Berlin and headed back over Stettin dropping our bombs.

Unfortunately, my fears of a tough raid were fully borne out. It was getting dark as we headed out over Cromer and we could see the folk on the promenade waving to us. They could not know that when they were having their evening meal or a pint in the local we would by fighting for our lives over Denmark. The route had been chosen because of the relatively light presence of guns, but there were plenty of night fighter bases, so we could expect lots of opposition. As we approached the coast of Denmark the crew were continually reporting fighter attacks on the bombers. I could see nothing of this because I was working on the chart behind the closed curtain. Suddenly, I heard Frank Ramsey the Rear Gunner, say to Johnny, the mid Upper Gunner, "There's a fighter coming up behind us!" Immediately, there was a loud rattle as both gunners opened fire.

Frank yelled, "Corkscrew starboard!"

The skipper instantly put the aircraft into a gut-wrenching dive for several hundred feet, climbed up again, then dived down again. This was the standard manoeuvre to avoid a fighter attack. After several minutes, which seemed an eternity, the gunners reported that they believed they had hit the fighter and driven it off.

Even while we were driving off the German Fighters, we were making progress towards the Eastern Coast of Denmark, and the strip of water called the Kattegatt that separates Denmark and Sweden. As we approached the Swedish Coast, I came from behind the navigator's curtain and had a look through the Astrodome to see what was going on. There seemed to be plenty of activity all around us. There were flashes of machine gun fire as aircraft fought each other, and in Sweden itself, I counted about six fires on the ground, most likely burning Lancasters. It was possible to see the lights of Sweden which was a neutral country and therefore entitled not to expect British bombers to be flying over. As far as I could see, we crossed the Swedish coast at the right place, we then turned in a south easterly direction and headed across Sweden for the Island of Bornholm.

The Baltic sea was relatively narrow and it was not a long flight to cross it to the north German Coast. This coast was heavily defended, because not only was the important port of Stettin there, but also, Germany's Rocket Research Station was nearby. As we approached we could see a really heavy barrage of anti-aircraft fire which we simply had to fly through and hope for the best. We crossed the German coast, headed towards Berlin and then turned back towards Stettin.

Bremen Docks Ablaze : Two Miles of Fire

TWO miles of Bremen docks were set ablaze by R.A.F. bombers when they attacked the port on Friday night and dropped 150,000 incendiaries. This was shown by reconnaissance pictures taken yesterday. The flames spread from the docks to the centre of the town.

A R.A.F. pilot who flew over the town yesterday reported that smoke rising to a great height was blowing into open country to a distance of about 60 miles.

Bremen was one of the two main objectives in an attack launched by more than 1,000 bombers, Sterkrade-Holten, which has about the sixth largest synthetic oil plant in the Ruhr, was the other chief target.

With more block-busters, Mosquitos also hit Berlin, Cologne, and other objectives in North-West Germany and the railway yard at Connantre, east of Paris, were also bombed and mines were laid in enemy waters. Four aircraft are missing.

Early yesterday a force of Lancasters attacked without loss an oil storage depot at La Pallice, on the west coast of France.

A Lancaster rear gunner, Sergt. C. Branch, of Birmingham, reported of the Bremen attack: "The markers dropped by the pathfinders were surrounded by innumerable fires. They were spreading as though someone was running round with a torch lighting up street after street. I have never seen fires spread so rapidly, nor have I seen such an intense concentration."

Although Bremen was heavily damaged in previous attacks, there were still important industrial areas to be bombed. It has recently gained in importance as a centre of the aircraft industry because the Focke-Wulf factory at Marienburg, in East Prussia, has recently been evacuated to Bremen.

Blow by R.A.F. aided Russia

SOME 500-750 Flying Fortresses, escorted by about two-thirds as many Mustangs, attacked Kiel and Bremen yesterday afternoon, bombing through cloud by means of instruments.

Meanwhile, answering a request of American ground forces, Ninth Air Force Havocs dropped bombs through ten-tenths cloud cover on an important fuel storage depot near Arques la Batille, about five miles southeast of Dieppe.

Forty-one out of the strong force of R.A.F. planes which had raided other German targets the previous night failed to return.

Making a 2,000-mile return trip through violent electrical storms, Lancasters struck deadly blows at Germany's Baltic bases of Stettin and Koenigsberg.

It was a bid to aid the Red Army massing only a hundred miles away. Germany has been frantically assembling supplies and reinforcements at these two great ports.

Down in Sweden

Our Stockholm correspondent cables that eight of our planes landed or crashed in Southern Sweden, only one Lancaster remaining intact, it is said.

Twenty-one British airmen have been found dead, and 22 alive, including some wounded.

The Swedish Official Agency states that an official protest is expected against the flight of the planes over Sweden.

Mosquitoes bombed Berlin and Hamburg the same night, while Beaufighters of Coastal Command played havoc with a small enemy convoy of five ships in the Heligoland Bight.

Need of Oil

The synthetic oil plant at Sterkrade-Holten was put out of action not long ago as a result of an attack by R.A.F. Bomber Command, but the enemy's need for oil is now so desperate that he has been forced to repair badly damaged plants in the Ruhr, even though he knows that there is every chance that they will be bombed again as soon as they have begun to produce.

Another important target hit was an oil storage depot at Rieme, in Belgium. Here, too, the bombing was also highly effective.

The enemy's air defences were completely at a loss, although the weather was entirely favourable for the night fighters, with clear skies over all the targets, apart from a little thin cloud in Belgium.

But the night fighters were out-manoeuvred. The timing and direction of last night's various attacks made the most of the great size of the area which the Luftwaffe has to defend.

First Attack

The first attack was on the railway yard at Connantre just before midnight, and the bombing was well concentrated. The oil storage depot at Rieme was attacked ten minutes later, and, at almost the same time, Lancasters and Halifaxes were over Bremen, nearly 400 miles away.

The Mosquito attack on Berlin, at 25 minutes past twelve, must have drawn still more of the defenders to the east, when half an hour later Bomber Command delivered its heavy attack at Sterkrade-Holten.

Other diversionary attacks added to the enemy's confusion.

Bomber Command's own night fighters, heavily armed Mosquitos, chased a number of enemy night fighters which did manage to get in touch with one of the attacking ces.

P-planes from Belgium

Halifaxes and Lancasters of R.A.F. Bomber Command, with fighter cover, yesterday attacked long-range weapon supply depots in Northern France

IT is believed that the enemy was using a new northerly flying-bomb base yesterday.

Most of the bombs which were launched in a series of short attacks appeared to come over the French coast between Calais and Dunkirk.

Observers think that most of them were discharged from sites in Belgium.

If the enemy attempts to continue the bombardment from Belgium (writes an Air Correspondent) it will mean that the bombs will have a greater sea distance to cover, and our aircraft patrol will have more time and space in which to attack them.

Free from A.A. fire

Our aircraft would also have an opportunity of tackling the bombs free from enemy A.A. fire.

South-Eastern and Eastern England are within range of flying-bomb attacks from the Belgian coast in the Ostend area, but clearing the Pas de Calais will rob the enemy of numerous sites that were prepared for constant and intensive attack on this country.

He is not likely to be so well prepared in Belgium and will not be encouraged to make expensive installations there in view of the threat of the advancing Allied armies.

From other sites yesterday or more or so of bombs came o hours. Formerly a sim usually came over in

We could not wait to get rid of our bombs and get out. As we approached the target, the bomb doors were open and the bomb aimer was guiding us over the target as usual when suddenly, the whole aircraft was lit up like daylight. We had been caught by the blue 'master searchlight beam' and in a matter of seconds we were 'coned' by many more searchlights. We were now a sitting target and the guns opened up on us.

The skipper yelled, "Drop those bloody bombs!"

We did.

He shut the bomb doors, pushed the nose of the Lancaster forward and for several thousand feet dived down the blue searchlight beam at over three hundred miles per hour. Quite honestly, I thought to myself at the time (and the others must have too) that this was the end. Either the guns would get us, or the aircraft would fall to pieces under the strain of the dive.

I am, of course, able to write this story because neither of these events happened. After the skipper had built up sufficient speed, he yanked the nose up and we shot out of the searchlight beam like a rocket into the welcome darkness over the Baltic sea.

After coming out of the dive it took me a few minutes to sort out where we were. I discovered we were heading along the Baltic Coast in the wrong direction. There many German night fighters about, so I calculated a course to take us near Malmo in southern Sweden, so that if we did run into any more trouble we could at least land in neutral Sweden.

We reached Sweden without any more trouble, turned westwards across Denmark and got shot at by AA guns in the suburbs of Copenhagen. They missed us, and we flew on across Denmark, crossed the Danish North Sea coast and headed back towards Mildenhall.

We flew low over the North Sea towards England, because we knew there was a danger of German fighters patrolling the area and by flying low we were clear of their radar. As we crossed the English coast, dawn began to break.

We had taken off at 2120 hours and landed back at Mildenhall at 0730 the following morning, a trip of over ten hours. Usually, when we had landed we managed some light-hearted conversation, but on this occasion, we realised we had been close to death and were lucky to be alive. We felt depressed and completely exhausted.

We lated discovered that the strong German defences had made the raid comparatively ineffective. They had shot down over 40 bombers and the Swedish government made strong protest to London about the violation of their neutrality by the RAF. However, I did have some good news, we were about to start on a week's leave. I could not sleep after the raid, so I packed a few things in a bag, picked up my leave pass, and began hitchhiking to Birmingham to see my girlfriend Eileen.

You will remember that I first met Eileen in 1940, soon after coming to Birmingham. We became firm friends and remain so over sixty years later. When I first met her, she worked in the Machine Accounting Department at the Wesleyan and General Assurance, whose head office was in the centre of Birmingham. Unfortunately, it was badly damaged during one of the big German raids on the city, and the staff had to be evacuated to the town of Malvern in

Worcestershire. About this time, all men and women of military age – from 17 to 35 – came under government regulations and were forced to do essential war work, either in the armed forces or in war-related civilian jobs. As a result of these regulations Eileen spent some time in the Ministry of Labour, dealing with the call-up of men and women into the armed forces. By 1943 almost all eligible people had been called up, so she was directed to the huge Aircraft Factory run by Vickers Armstrong at Castle Bromwich near Birmingham where Lancasters and Spitfires were assembled. This was located about ten miles from her home in Moseley. Transport was provided by a special bus, which left at 6 am and returned at 5 pm. There were about 20,000 people employed there. Eileen worked as a Technical Liaison Clerk in the Drawing Office, dealing with modifications to the Lancaster Bomber. As she walked through the factory she could see lines of the Lancasters and Spitfires. The factory seemed like a small town, with its own road network, crossings etc. Most people ate their meals in a huge canteen. On occasions lunch-time concerts were arranged, and many well known film actors, dance bands, and so on, came along to entertain, with the idea of keeping up the morale of the workers and telling them what a crucial part they were playing in the war effort. As a further help, both British and American aircrews came along to give talks about their experiences. Every effort was made to boost production and not least of these ideas was the playing of 'music while you work' for half-an-hour during the morning and afternoon, played over loud speakers from Radio Broadcasts by the BBC. Through Eileen, I knew her bosses, who were in charge of the Drawing Office, and knowing that I was flying on Lancasters, they were always keen to ask my opinion on the modifications they were making. Unfortunately, I knew too little about the mechanics of a Lancaster to tell them how good the changes were. All I could say, was that it was a fine aircraft.

When I met Eileen at lunchtime on my first leave from Mildenhall we went to a nearby cafe for a snack. It was about 12.55 pm and the radio in the cafe was switched on for the 1 o'clock news. Invariably, in those days, the news bulletin commenced with the words, "Last night, aircraft of RAF Bomber Command attacked targets in Germany..." and would then give a list of targets attacked and the number of aircraft lost. On this particular occasion, the newsreader said, "The main target attacked was the important North German port of Stettin. From the night's operations, 45 of our aircraft were missing."

I remarked to Eileen, "A mere eleven hours ago, I was involved in that raid and was very nearly shot down, yet here I am, having a cup of tea and cake with you in the comfort of this cafe!" What a strange world we were living in.

We had become engaged in June 1943 and decided on this leave that if I survived flying with Bomber Command we would get married. The Heads of Eileen's department were always considerate and they allowed her a few days holiday when I was on leave. We spent a very enjoyable time together.

After a week's leave, I felt more relaxed and returned to Mildenhall to meet up with the rest of the crew. On the face of it we all seemed back to our relaxed and jovial selves.

Date	Hour	Aircraft Type and No.	Pilot	Duty
Oct 2		LANCASTER F	F/O BAXTER	NAVIGATOR
Oct 5		LANCASTER G	F/O BAXTER	NAVIGATOR
6		LANCASTER G	F/O BAXTER	NAVIGATOR
14		LANCASTER G	F/O BAXTER	NAVIGATOR
14		LANCASTER G	F/O BAXTER	NAVIGATOR
18		LANCASTER G	F/O BAXTER	NAVIGATOR
22		LANCASTER D	F/O BAXTER	NAVIGATOR
23		LANCASTER D	F/O BAXTER	NAVIGATOR
28		LANCASTER B	F/O BAXTER	NAVIGATOR
30		LANCASTER D	F/O BAXTER	NAVIGATOR
31		LANCASTER D	F/O BAXTER	NAVIGATOR

My log book, showing various ops over Germany.

	Time carried forward :—	177.06	116.45
OCTOBER			
		Flying Times	
	REMARKS (including results of bombing, gunnery, exercises, etc.)	Day	Night
	FORMATION G.H.	2·30	
6po.	SAARBRUECKEN		5·55
6po.	DORTMUND — hit by flak.		5·40
6po	DUISBURG. (Happy Valley)	4·20	
6po	DUISBURG		5·15
6po	BONN — hit by incendiaries	4·40	
6po	NEUSS (Dusseldorf)	4·25	
6po.	ESSEN (KRUPP's works) (hit by flak)		5·15
6po.	COLOGNE (Marshalling yards)	4·25	
6po.	WESSELING (Oil plant Near Cologne)	4·30	
6po.	BOTTROP (Oil plant Near Gladbach)	4·40	

Total Flying for October

Total Day   29.30

Total Night   22·05

Total   51·35

Certified Correct.

A.J. Phillips F/Lt O.C. 'A' Flight

	TOTAL TIME ...		

However, deep down, I myself was thinking that if our experiences on our first few operations were typical, we would be lucky to survive.

However, in September, we had a stroke of luck, as far as targets were concerned. From the beginning of the war, the main objective for Bomber Command, joined later by the American 8th Air Force, was to destroy industrial targets in Germany. When it was decided in 1944 for the British and American armies to invade Europe, the Bomber Forces were used to destroy communications in North West France thus assisting in the invasion.

By August 1944 the bombing of Germany had been resumed and the armies had advanced across France and into Belgium. The supply lines for these armies stretched hundreds of miles from Normandy and it was essential that some French Channel Ports should be captured immediately. These ports were, Le Havre, Calais, Boulogne and Dieppe. Realising their importance, the Germans had heavily fortified them. To avoid loss of life by the army, and to speed up their capture, the full force of Bomber Command was used to bomb them into submission.

We found ourselves as part of this force, bombing Le Havre three times and Calais twice in September. You can imagine our relief at these relatively easy targets, after our experiences over Germany the previous month.

However, there were two interesting instances worth recalling in September. On Sunday 17th September in the morning, we were called into the Wing Commander's Office and told that the wife of one of the ground crew was expecting a baby imminently and was liable to have complications. We were told to fly the husband to Woodvale near Southport which was close to where his wife was in hospital. As we flew near Peterborough on the way to Southport, we saw literally hundreds of planes and gliders flying towards the East Anglian coast – a most impressive sight. We thought they must be on training exercise, but later that day a news bulletin informed us that what we had seen was in fact the largest airborne invasion ever mounted – operation Market-Garden – the landing of airborne forces in Holland.

We duly arrived at Woodvale, and parked near an American Flying Fortress. Having chatted to the American crew for a while we decided to inspect each others aircraft. The main difference I remember was that the American aircraft was very heavily armoured with .50 machine guns, but had a small bomb bay, whereas the Lancaster was lightly armoured but had a huge bomb bay.

The second memorable incident in September was a raid on a very large synthetic oil plant in Germany just north of the Ruhr. Bomber Command almost always attacked Germany in darkness, but this raid was carried out at dusk and it was therefore possible to see the Lancasters and Halifaxes on their way to the target. The anti-aircraft fire was extremely heavy and as I stood in the Astrodome looking around I saw two Lancasters completely blown up, about a quarter of a mile away. Where a few seconds earlier there had been two aircraft with fourteen men on board, there were two clouds of black smoke with debris all over the place. This image has stuck in my mind ever since, and the knowledge

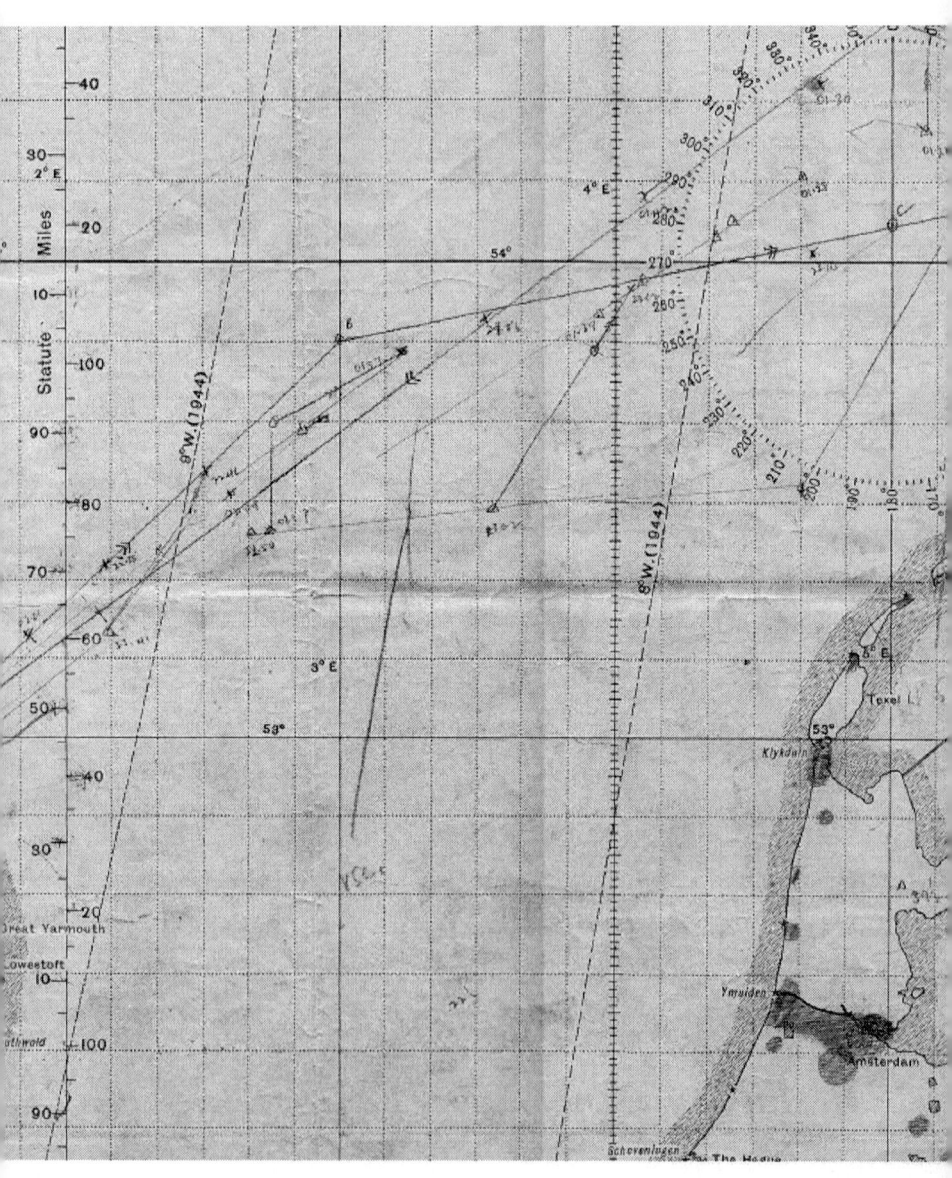

One of my Navigator's charts, showing the route plotted across the North Sea to attack Bremen.

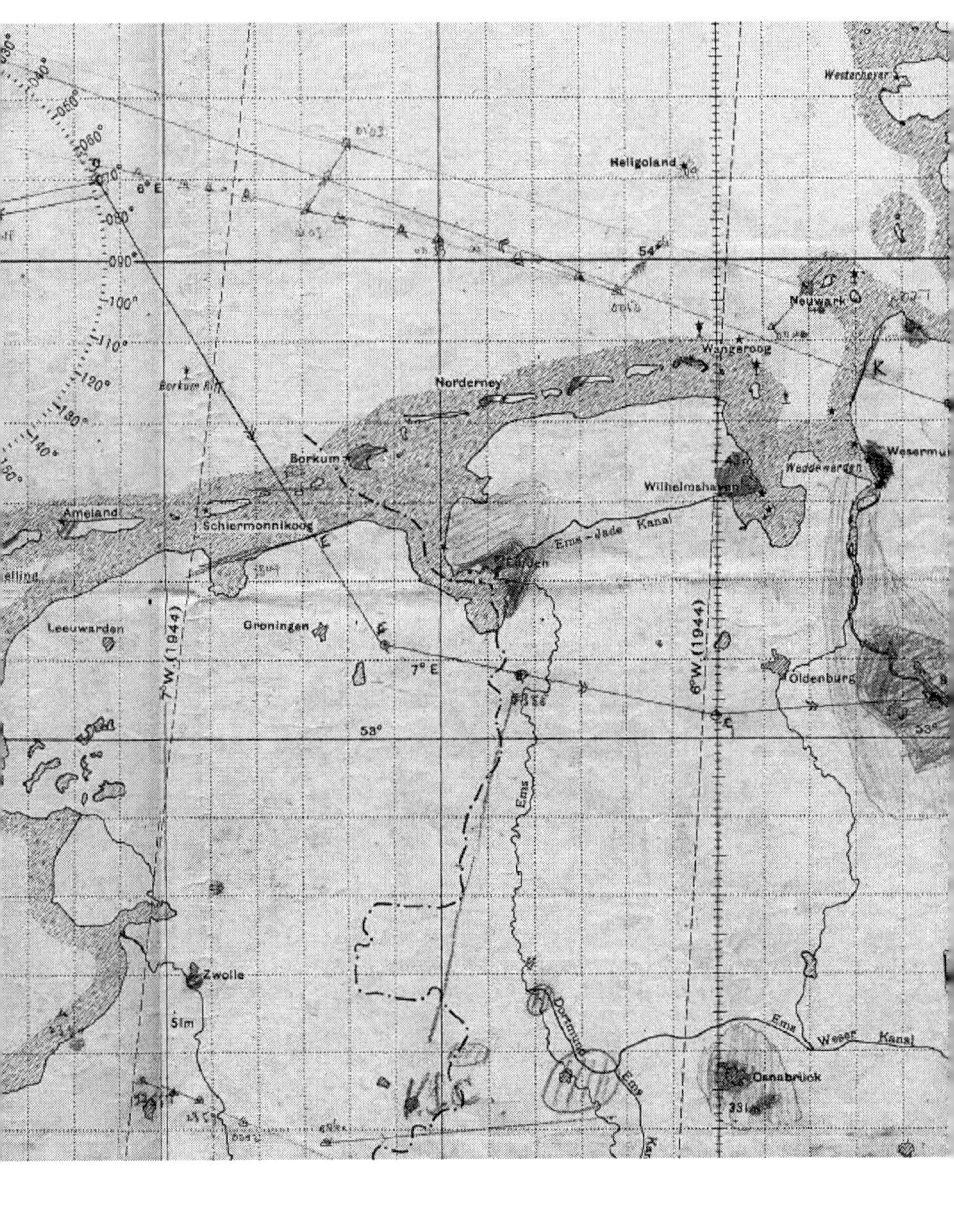

that one could die instantly was always at the back of my mind whenever I flew afterwards. This seems very naive – obviously a direct hit on the bomb load would blow the aircraft up – but all my flying so far had been at night, when there were so many flashes, bombs and searchlights that it was impossible to tell exactly what was happening.

We realised that as the armies advanced across Europe we would run out of easy targets and we would soon be attacking Germany again, and sure enough, in early October, we began bombing Germany's industrial heartland of the Ruhr, especially their synthetic oil plants. This was recognised as the most heavily defended area in the world and we knew that we were in for a tough time.

We started off with a heavy attack on Dortmund. This particular raid sticks in my mind because as we approached the target with bomb doors open, there was a sudden loud crack, and a nasty piece of shrapnel came through the floor of the aircraft, between the wireless operator and me. It must have gone several feet in to the air before dropping on to the floor. It was very alarming, it measured about six inches by three and about one inch thick. This could have caused a bad injury, but even worse (we discovered when we returned to base) it had passed very near to the bombs before they were dropped. Another lucky escape.

George Brooker, our Wireless Operator, measured the distance between the hole in the floor and our position in the aircraft. We calculated that George was slightly nearer, and he therefore kept the piece as a souvenir, and used it to get free drinks in the local pub!

After this opening raid, we returned to Germany every few days until we had completed our thirty one operations by December 1944. Some of them were trouble free, others we were extremely fortunate to survive. For example, one notable daylight raid during November was to Bonn. The flack was very heavy as we headed towards the target a few miles ahead. Suddenly, we saw a Lancaster about five hundred feet above us, who obviously did not like the look of the gunfire and dropped his bombs without regard for the fact that we were underneath. There was a terrible clattering as incendiaries hit the wings of our aircraft. We just could not believe what was going on! When we returned to base the ground crew found several unexploded incendiaries. This ranked as one of our luckiest escapes.

Some idea of the scale of the Bomber Command effort to end the war can be taken from the fact that the big inland port of Duisburg on the river Rhine was bombed twice in sixteen hours. We were woken at about 3 am for briefing, dropped five and half tons of bombs at dawn, and then, on our return, the aircraft was prepared for another raid which took place that evening.

In the meantime, the American 8th airforce with its Flying Fortresses and Liberators, heavily escorted by fighters, bombed targets in Germany by daylight. As they were also based in East Anglia it was usual to see the Americans returning from bombing Germany as we set off. The idea of these huge attacks was to force Germany to surrender and to reduce the casualties to the British and American armies.

Date	Hour	Aircraft Type and No.	Pilot	Duty
DEC 14		LANCASTER G	P/O Baxter	Navigator

My log book entry showing the final tally at the end of our 'tour of duty' with Bomber Command.

	Time carried forward :—	250.15	1438.0

REMARKS (including results of bombing, gunnery, exercises, etc.)	Flying Times	
	Day	Night
6/7. OBERHAUSEN	4.30	

END OF FIRST TOUR OF OPERATIONS ON 622 SQ.

(30 OPERATIONS)

Total Flying on 622 Sqdn MILDENHALL

OPERATIONAL	Day	100.35	100.35
			30.50
	Night	50.40	69.45
	Total	154.15	
OTHER	Day	19.00	
	Night	4.20	
	Total	23.20	

Sgd. A.J. Phillips Ofr.

for O.C.

622 Squadron

OFFICER COMMANDING
No. 622 SQUADRON R.A.F.

TOTAL TIME ...		

In addition to the bombing of the Ruhr we were also briefed to carry out 'gardening' – this being an RAF term for operations involving the dropping of mines in enemy estuaries and harbours to sink their shipping. This was carried out by flying at very low levels above the sea. My stomach turned over at the thought of it. Fortunately, these operations were cancelled at the last minute owing to bad weather, and instead we were sent back to the Ruhr.

Apart from a week's leave every three weeks, we had little time to relax. Whenever there was an evening off we went on the RAF bus to Newmarket where we drowned our sorrows in the local. Here we frequently met American Air Crews and we talked to them about flying. A few of them were bombastic and were always ready to argue and fight, but in general, most were very nice brave men for whom we had the highest admiration. They had similar regard for the work of Bomber Command.

When the American Air Force returned to their bases after a raid, the casualties on board required ambulances to race up to the aircraft when it landed.

As we got to November, the number of our operations steadily increased and by mid November we realised there was a good chance of us finishing. It was always said that the most dangerous period for a bomber crew was the first five operations and the last five, because of tension. Although none of us said anything, photographs taken at this time

Opposite page: My crew, after completing a tour of duty. L to R: George Brooker (W/Op), Les Parsons (navigator), Johnny Scoular (mid-upper gunner), Mac Baxter (pilot), 'Hoppy' Hopkinson (bomb aimer), Frank Ramsey (rear gunner), Ted Rossiter (flight engineer).

showed us to be looking ten years older than when we had started our 'tour'. We were pale and could not raise a smile between us. On the last few operations we were hit by flak but fortunately, the plane was not seriously damaged.

Then one morning in December 1944 we and another crew were called into the Wing Commander's office and were told that we had completed the number of operations required. He asked if anyone would like to volunteer to do any more but no one stepped forward. "OK," the Wing Commander said, "Well done. In two days we shall send you on indefinite leave until you are posted to more training duties, so you can forget flying duties for the next six months at least."

That night we had a big party in the mess – as we had planned to do the previous August – and then went off on leave thinking that all our RAF problems were over.

How wrong we were!

CHAPTER VII

A Posting Overseas

By December 1944 I had trained as a Navigator and completed a tour of 31 battle operations, mostly over Germany. In December 1944 Eileen and I were married; we were both 21 years old. When we returned from honeymoon there was a telegram from Mildenhall waiting for me, saying that I must be prepared for overseas service. This came as quite a shock, as usually when a crew had completed a tour over Germany they were given six months rest from flying. This rest period was usually spent passing on your experiences to new crews. After being home seven days, I received another telegram, telling me to report back to Mildenhall on 1st January 1945.

I reported back as instructed and found the rest of my crew, plus seven or eight other crews who had all received similar telegrams. It was rumoured that we were being sent to the Bahamas – where there was a large aircrew training base – to join the training staff. Rumours were also rife that we were to spend two weeks leave in New York en-route, which sounded most attractive.

Before going overseas, we were supposed to be examined to see if we were medically fit. We were duly seen by the Station Medical Officer, who duly arrived at 2 pm, having been drinking in the Officers Mess for the previous two hours.

His 'examination' consisted of listening to the heartbeat (through the shirt) and saying, "If you're as good when you get back home as you are now, you'll be OK!" So with that, two or three days later, we were sent to Morecambe in Lancashire, which was a large Personnel Dispersal centre for RAF members being sent on overseas service.

We were billeted in an old-fashioned boarding house in West End Road. The lady owning and running it was a typical Lancashire seaside Landlady, more used to taking in Cotton Mill workers for their week's summer holiday than young airmen. Her name was Mrs Miller. The weather in January 1945 was bitterly cold and coal for heating was very scarce. We used to go to bed in all our clothes and we would tease Mrs Miller by shouting 'Coalman!' which would get her running to the door – but she took it in good spirit.

We spent about a week at Morecambe, during which time we were issued with 'tropical kit'. The RAF Storekeeper issued the kit in a kit bag without any attempt to measure any of us. He said to me, "You look a medium size." The kit consisted of two pairs of khaki shorts, two shirts, one bush hat, two pairs of knee-length socks and two pairs of pants.

While in Morecambe the group of airmen that came with us from Mildenhall were given a draft number. While walking round the town I met a young man who I had known in Civvy Street by the name of Tony Neale. He had joined the RAF and trained as a pilot on Liberators in the Bahamas. He told me he also was on an overseas draft and his draft number was near my own. He also told me he was expecting to go to the Far East, and for the first time I became convinced that this was our true destination and that the rumour that we were going to the Bahamas was just that – a rumour.

The thought of going to India filled us all with foreboding. You have to appreciate that before 1939 very few people had been away from their own towns or villages. It was exceptional in those days even to have a week's holiday at, say Blackpool, Morecambe or Weston-Super-Mare. People's only knowledge of the outside world came from school Geography lessons, newspapers, or the cinema. These sources left plenty of room for the imagination and India, in my head, was full of dangerous snakes, crocodiles and tigers.

On a Monday morning in mid January 1945 we assembled, with hundreds of others at 6 am on Morecambe station where we boarded a troop train. After several hours travelling we called in at some docks, which turned out to be the Gladstone Docks at Liverpool. Beside the quay was moored a huge ship. We climbed the gang-plank and discovered that the ship was named the *Cape Town Castle* and was to be our home for the next three weeks. This ship was one of several Union Castle liners which in peacetime had been on a regular passenger service between Southampton and Capetown, South Africa. Before 1939 there were very few passenger airline services and most long-distance passenger transport was by sea. Each country had its own passenger liners and at the outbreak of war these ships were commandeered by the government and converted into Troop Ships. The *Cape Town Castle* weighed 28,000 tons and was converted to carry about 5,000 troops. It was filled from top to bottom and you just hoped that you were not on the bottom. These troop ships travelled quickly (over 20 knots) and this speed helped to reduce the risk of being sunk by German submarines, although there were some instances of troop ships being sunk by torpedoes, losing all on board. The troop ships generally travelled in convoy, supported by Royal Navy Destroyers. The only troop ships regularly travelling on their own were the 80,000 ton *Queen Mary* and *Queen Elizabeth* which could both travel at 30 knots. When we boarded the *Cape Town Castle* we were very fortunate to find ourselves allocated to the top deck of the boat.

The first class dining room had been converted into one huge area of sleeping accommodation comprised of metal fold-away beds, with about four beds in each tier, one above the other, which gave little space to get dressed in. Fortunately, this room led out onto the open deck, so it was possible to get into the fresh air quickly. This was marvellous when we got into the Mediterranean and the Red Sea. We used to feel very sorry for the troops down below, mainly army, without any natural light or fresh air. I cannot recall too much about the food we had, but can remember eating plenty of bread, corned beef and kippers. As Air Crew we were privileged to have a separate dining room, whereas the other ranks had to eat and sleep in the same area on long wooden tables, which were called 'mess' tables.

On the quay next to the *Cape Town Castle* was a huge warehouse which seemed as tall as the ship. Every morning we walked onto the open deck expecting to be at sea, but instead saw the frost covered roof of the warehouse. As well as frost there was thick fog in the Mersey and we were unable to set sail. These conditions went on day after day and we began to think we were never going to leave Liverpool. This had gone on for six days, when suddenly, at about 10.30 am on a Sunday morning there was great activity on the quayside, with the gangplank being taken up, and we knew were about to commence our long journey. What a strange feeling it was to see the ship slowly moving away from the quayside. It was about 12 noon when the ship went through the dock gates and into the Mersey.

At the dock entrance we saw a solitary man pushing his bike and waving us 'goodbye'. He was most likely on his way home to Sunday dinner. In the Mersey there were three or four other ships waiting to depart with us. We all set sail at about 2 pm, accompanied by a Royal Navy Destroyer.

We sailed up past the Isle of Man and through the Channel between Scotland and Ireland. We could see very clearly the snow on the mountains of the Lake District and Southern Scotland. We sailed north up the Scottish Coast for several hours and then turned west and into the central Atlantic, away from the German Submarine bases.

When we left Liverpool, the sea was quite calm, but as we headed into the Atlantic the weather changed completely and we headed straight into an Atlantic gale with mountainous seas. We awoke at about 4 am to the sound of banging, rattling and rocking. The ship was being tossed about like a cork.

We air crews were given the job of looking after the RAF other ranks. I was given the job of ensuring that one of the Mess Decks was clean and tidy, all the bedding was folded and stacked away correctly, that the toilet was clean, and the knives, forks and plates were clean.

At about 7.30 am I went down to the Mess Deck on my first day of duty. Some men were just eating their breakfast while others were being sick were they stood, others were queuing for the toilet. It was a right shambles. Although I was not seasick myself, the smell of sick, sweaty feet and kippers was quite nauseating. It took until 11 am to get the place in some sort of order.

The storm lasted about 36 hours, after which time we turned south and the weather started to improve. We did physical training daily to keep fit. This was done on the upper deck and we could see the other ships in the convoy quite clearly. We could also see the accompanying Destroyers which from time to time seemed to completely disappear. The convoy followed a zig-zag course to help to avoid attacks. It was interesting to see dolphins and porpoises following the ship, a beautiful sight.

After heading south for several days, we turned East towards Gibraltar. About 100 miles from there, the convoy split up. Some went to Freetown but we went to Gibraltar and stayed there for 24 hours, although no-one was allowed off the ship.

At this stage of the war (January 1945) Italy had been defeated and German and Italian submarines cleared from the Mediterranean. It was considered safe, therefore, to send ships heading for India, without an escort. After a day in Gibraltar we headed for the Suez Canal along the coast of North Africa. As we neared the canal, the weather became much warmer. One day we were ordered to parade in tropical kit. This was the first time our tropical kit had been opened, and the sight of everyone in this gear sent us into fits of laughter. Although the material was of high quality, the sizing was hopeless. I had a pair of shorts that came below my knees and the shirt was miles too long, as were the sleeves. Almost everyone had similar problems. George Brooker, our Wireless Operator, considered himself to be good with a needle and cotton. He had been issued with shorts that were much too tight, so he cut down the back seams and sewed a piece in, and so ended up with a most peculiar pair of shorts, causing peals of laughter.

Needless to say, when we arrived in India, we sold off the kit to the Indians and bought much smarter looking clothes. After another day's sailing we arrived at Port Said in Egypt at the northern end of the Suez Canal. As we approached the harbour, we passed a very imposing statue of the Frenchman Ferdinand De Lesseps who had built the canal a hundred years earlier. This statue was demolished by the Egyptians when they took over the Canal.

On entering the harbour we joined a queue of ships waiting to be taken down the Canal by an experienced pilot. We waited 24 hours for our turn. During this time we were besieged by 'bum boats'. These were small boats, usually rowing, manned by local inhabitants, carrying varieties of wares. They would pull up near to the ship and prices were bargained with them. Goods were received by means of a basket on a rope and money paid over in the same way. I bought two handbags in this way, for one pound each. There were also young children in the boats, they would encourage us to throw coins in the water and they would dive in to retrieve them. This was all new to us and we found it entertaining.

We slowly entered the Canal and headed for the Red Sea. Quite a strange experience, the ship was so high up in the water and you could see miles upon miles of desert on either side. The Suez Canal passes through two lakes called the Great Bitter Lake and the Small Bitter Lake. We were surprised that the ship dropped anchor in the Great Bitter and we were allowed ashore for a few hours. We played football against the local British Army teams. Some of these men had been away from England for five years, and were most anxious to have news of home. We boarded the ship again after several hours and felt much better for the change.

We soon entered the Red Sea and it became very hot, extremely so. Near the southern end of the Red Sea was a refuelling station called Aden, where we stopped to refuel. This only took a few hours, and we then headed for Bombay across the Arabian Sea. The heat was terrific and we were delighted that we were on the upper deck. The heat on the bottom deck, we were told, was unbearable. Being able to go on the deck at night, it was fascinating to see the shining phosphorous on the surface of the sea, thrown up by the ship, as it cut through the water. After a few more days we arrived in Bombay, having sailed for about three weeks.

We disembarked, and were put onto lorries and taken to a transit camp at Worli, a very pleasant suburb of Bombay. A few days later when we had settled in to the Transit Camp we went into the centre of Bombay to look around. We were appalled by the scenes of poverty. People seemed to be living on the streets which were full of beggars both young and old, all shouting 'backsheesh' which means "give us something for nothing". As we approached the centre of Bombay we saw that people lived in 'shacks'. The smells were far worse than anything I had encountered in England. There were flies everywhere. What an awful disgrace that people should have to live like that.

On our second day at Worli the ten aircrews, 70 men altogether, were told to report to a senior RAF Officer, who said that they had no knowledge of crews being sent from England. This was not an unusual circumstance in the RAF. We explained to him that we had been told that we were being sent to the Bahamas as Instructors, and that in any case, were due for six months rest from flying duties with Bomber Command. He promised to talk to his senior officer, an Air Commodore, who would speak to us tomorrow. This meeting took place. The Air Commodore was sympathetic and agreed that we were entitled to a rest from flying. He gave the following two choices:

1.   We could take our rest, in which case we would be separated from the men in our crew and given the worst jobs available or...

2.   We could stay together as a crew and convert to fly a Liberator bomber and resume operations over Burma as quickly as possible. (In the Far East they were short of heavy bomber crews and wanted to make use of our experience.)

He gave us one hour to make up our minds. It did not take us long to decide. We would stay together as a crew and take our chances flying rather than be posted individually god-knows-where in a strange country.

The A/C seemed very pleased at our decision and said that, as soon as possible, we would be sent on a Liberator conversion course at Kilar near Bangalore, Southern India – a three day rail journey from Bombay. It was now the end of February, our journey having taken taken six weeks since leaving Liverpool.

We said goodbye to Tony Neale and the other friends we had made on the journey who were already trained to fly Liberators. They were due to be sent to an operational squadron in Bengal.

We had to join a troop train at Poona, a military camp about one hundred miles from Bombay. We travelled from Bombay on the ordinary train and changed stations about halfway at a small village. We had three hours to wait, so it gave us time to have a look around. It was a market day and there were many stalls selling all kinds of wares. Among the food stalls there was one selling sliced melons and I said to my friend, "I didn't think melons were black." As we got closer we realised that they were covered in black flies.

Soon it was time to catch our train. After about two hours we arrived at Poona where we joined a very large troop train taking Army and RAF personnel to Bangalore, a journey of about three and a half days.

On the troop train there was a compartment for every four people which contained two wooden benches and two luggage racks. The sleeping accommodation was on the benches or luggage racks. I was with the wireless operator and the two gunners, and we drew lots for the sleeping accommodation. I was lucky enough to get a bench seat, while the wireless operator had to make do with the luggage rack. During normal travelling we would all sit on the wooden seat. On this occasion, George the wireless operator was wearing very short shorts and when he stood up after two hours, the backs of his legs were raw red where the wood bugs had bitten him.

"I'm not going to sit on these bloody seats," he said, "I'm off to bed!" (i.e. the luggage rack). He then coated himself with anti mosquito cream and with our help climbed onto the luggage rack. It looked as though it was going to collapse at any minute. We covered him with the mosquito net, said goodnight and waited for his reaction. After about 30 minutes he emerged, red faced and heavily perspiring, complaining that there was little oxygen up there. His final solution was to put on long trousers and huddle on the seat in the corner.

Another unusual item was the toilet, which consisted of a hole in the floor with two metal rails at the side to hold on to. As can be imagined, it caused great difficulty and considerable amusement until we got the hang of it.

On the way to Bangalore the train stopped at a station called Belgaum. The four of us had just eaten a tin of pears and I was about to throw away the tin, when an old man came up with outstretched hands, pleading for the empty tin. When I gave it to him he looked absolutely thrilled. The picture of someone getting so much pleasure from so little has remained with me ever since.

Continuing on our journey, we passed through areas of jungle which came very close to the railway line and it was possible to see monkeys swinging in trees. Then we heard shots being fired from some parts of the train. Apparently some of the troops were finding amusement firing at the poor monkeys, which we found disgusting.

After two and a half days on the train we arrived at Bangalore, where we should have been met by RAF lorries to take us to the Kolar Air Base. However, these had not turned up and we were told to report back to the railway station in two hours time. This gave us a chance to have a look around the town. It was much more pleasant than Bombay; there was not so much humidity, the streets were cleaner and there were not so many people begging.

When we returned to the station the RAF lorries were waiting for us and we quickly did the 20 miles or so to the air base. As I recall, the accommodation there was good. Each crew had its own hut, which was spacious enough for eight of us. It was well ventilated and in spite of the heat was pleasantly cool. A small section of our hut was sectioned off for a Flt/Sgt Engine Fitter, one of the permanent staff. He had an old-fashioned manual gramophone on which he was always playing his favourite record, 'Down in the Valley' by the Andrews Sisters. We used to hear this every morning, noon and night, which drove us barmy. Whenever I hear this record it immediately triggers memories of this chap and his wind-up gramophone.

At Kolar we had our first taste of being looked after by Indian servants. We had a little lad who we called Jimmy. He was about thirteen years of age and he lived in one of the nearby villages. He cleaned our shoes, made the beds and generally tidied up, took and collected our laundry to the Dhobi wallah. Jimmy was liked by us all. I cannot remember what we paid him, but at the time, it was thought to be quite generous. After a few weeks we were upset to find that he had stolen money and goods from us, and had run off. The temptation had proved too much for him, and realising his own poverty, and that of his family, we could hardly blame him. Our next job was to find another bearer. This time he was a thirty year old Indian named Chowasi. We had to pay him more money, but he looked after us really well, especially when this involved purchasing goods for us from the outside, making sure we got good value for money. He told us he was having a struggle supporting two wives, one in northern India and the other in Kolar!

We enjoyed being looked after, as one can imagine, and this brought back memories of a conversation I had had a few months earlier. When Eileen and I were on our honeymoon in December 1944 (when I had no idea that I would go to India) we spent a few days with her cousin Kitty and husband George Muir who was a Marine Engineer. George had spent much of the 1930s in Calcutta working on steamships transporting people up the Hoogly River. In 1935 Kitty was one of the first lady passengers to fly the Imperial Airways route to Calcutta, where she married George. They had a fabulous lifestyle with every luxury including lavish entertainment and lots of servants. When I talked to George he was very upset at having to return to England just before the war started.

He said to me, "The worst thing the British did in India was to educate the Indians, as this gave them the skill to govern their own country, which will mean the end of British rule." Although I did not comment on this to him, I felt privately shocked, but in Kolar I was to see for myself the lifestyle he regretted losing.

Kolar was the centre of the Indian gold mines and most of the managers and senior staff were British. They had a very comfortable lifestyle with their wives and families. The wives had set up a canteen for RAF personnel and it was opened every weekend. It was about ten miles from the RAF station and the RAF provided free transport to the canteen. When not flying we used to visit it regularly, and this made a pleasant change. We used to sit and read books and newspapers, write letters, listen to gramophone records and they provided very appetising sandwiches etc.

The English folk we talked to in the canteen were most interesting and anxious to hear news from back home. They were curious to know how long we thought the war would last. They confirmed what a high standard of living they were enjoying and said that they were not looking forward to returning to England when their contracts ended. It made me think of what George had said.

In addition to our visits to the canteen, our other off duty relaxation was a visit to the camp cinema, which was run by Indians. This was an unforgettable experience. There was always a long queue waiting to go in, and the queue was patrolled by local Indians selling large bags of monkey nuts which everyone bought. When the films were boring, which they often were, the monkeynut shells provided useful ammunition to throw at each other. I saw many a show end in chaos. The Indian projectionists did not help matters, as they frequently got the reels in a muddle, so it was not unusual to see the end of the film first, or have the projector break down altogether. Most were cowboy films, so there was plenty of opportunity to cheer and stamp our feet! This may sound rather silly, but at the time it gave us a good laugh and did much to relieve the tension and homesickness we were feeling.

As a special treat we were occasionally given an exhibition by a snake charmer. Snakes are my pet aversion, and I am sure many others felt the same. We sat down on the sand in the middle of our camp in a circle, about twenty five yards from the snake charmer. He brought in a large basket, took off the lid, brought out his pipe or tin whistle and started to play. Slowly, but surely, out of the basket came a hooded cobra (deadly poisonous) swaying its head from side to side in time to the music. Suddenly, it made a quick dart at the snake charmer. In a flash we all jumped back about ten yards in complete terror but to his credit the snake charmer remained calm and re-established control over the snake. Perhaps it was all part of the show...

A 99 Squadron Liberator on display at the Cosford Air Museum.

CHAPTER VIII

A Liberator Over Burma

The purpose of our posting to Kolar was to convert us from flying the British-built Lancaster to the American-built Liberator bomber, with which the RAF Far Eastern Strategic Air Force was equipped. Until I had arrived at Kolar I had never seen the Liberator, except in pictures, and there were many important differences between it and the Lancaster.

When we approached the Liberator on the ground one of the chaps said to me "isn't it an ugly looking aeroplane. It looks like a piece of slab cake!" This was in reference to its bulky appearance compared with the sleek lines of both the Lancaster and the American Flying Fortress. However, the Liberator was a very successful and versatile aircraft. It was used as a bomber, submarine hunter, for convoy protection, as a troop carrier and for aerial reconnaissance. More than 13,000 of them were built altogether. It was powered by four Pratt & Witney Twin Wasp engines which had a good reputation for reliability. This was very important in view of the long operations (eighteen to twenty hours) we were to undertake in this aircraft.

There were several differences which we spotted straight away. The Liberator had a tricycle undercarriage, that is, one wheel under each wing and one wheel under the nose. At the time, this was most unusual, as aircraft generally had a tail wheel as well as the wheels under the wing. We found this made for easier take off and landing, because the aircraft was already in the flying position on the ground, as are all aircraft today. (The first job with a tail-wheeled aircraft when taking off was to get the tail off the ground, and it took quite a bit of runway to do this.) The second remarkable thing about a Liberator was that the front and back of the aircraft were joined together by a steel 'catwalk'. On either side of the catwalk, the bombs were mounted and were protected by roller shutter doors. This meant that when you walked down the catwalk from front to back you could actually touch the bombs, and when the bomb doors were open it was possible to see the ground and to watch the bombs go down. On some occasions I stood on the edge of the bomb bay and watched them go down. How I ever did this I will never know, because today I can hardly climb a few steps without feeling peculiar! In every other bomber I had flown in, the bomb bays and bombs were underneath the floor of the aircraft and so you never saw them.

Because the Liberator flew on operations so far over enemy territory, there was no possibility of having a fighter escort. It was therefore heavily armoured and carried five gunners in the hope of beating off any attack. Our first job was to increase our Lancaster crew by three. Our Liberator crew became:

'Mac' Baxter*	Captain
Bob Mackay	Second Pilot
Les Parsons*	Navigator
Frank Carter	Bomb Aimer

George Brooker*	Wireless Operator
Frank Ramsey*	Rear Gunner
Johnny Scoular*	Mid Upper Gunner
Tommy Riley	Ball Gunner
Larry Sayce	Waist Gunner
Tony Osborne	Waist Gunner

*These were former Lancaster crew.

In most aircraft, the navigator's position is close to the pilot, but in the Liberator it was in the nose of the aircraft, so after take off the navigator had to crawl through a narrow tunnel to reach his position. However, one advantage was that it gave good visibility. While it could easily give a feeling of claustrophobia, it was nothing compared to the ball-gunner's position, whereby the gunner was put into the ball and then lowered below the aircraft by one of the other gunners.

Having got our bearings around the camp we had a few days ground lectures before becoming airborne.

On the 19 March 1945 we took off, together with an instructor for our first flight in a Liberator. This was exactly fifteen weeks since we had stepped out of a Lancaster for the last time – so much for our six months rest from flying! By now, we had become so experienced it only needed about two hours practice before taking the Liberator up on our own. We stayed at Kolar for some five weeks or so, and in this time, we did many cross-country flights around India. These flights generally took about six hours, and included practice formation flying with other Liberators, practice bombing and firing the guns at targets in the Indian Ocean. This time of the year the weather in southern India was beautiful. I seem to remember that every day was cloudless and splendid for flying. As far as navigation was concerned there was clear visibility for map reading and it was possible to see the sun, moon, and the stars to check the aircraft position. There were some navigational aids available but these were unreliable. Altogether we did roughly sixty hours flying from Kolar, and by the end of April we were told we were efficient enough to join an operational squadron in northern India. Thus, we were sent to join 99 squadron at Dhubulia, a base about sixty miles north of Calcutta.

There were four crews posted there, and this involved a three an half day journey by rail. The first part of the journey was by night train from Kolar station to Madras. A special carriage was reserved for the RAF on the Bangalore to Madras night train express. We were taken to Kolar station by RAF lorry and we waited around on the platform. It was a hot and sticky night and we wandered around the station. I went into a waiting room and there huddled in a corner were two small Indian boys, fast asleep. Flies were buzzing around them. They seemed to have been abandoned and it was a sight I have never been able to forget. We felt helpless at being unable to do anything for them. About five minutes later our train pulled in. Sadly, we got on. If the little boys survived they would now be about sixty. We pulled in at Madras at nine o clock on the following morning. As our train was not due to depart until late afternoon we had a few hours to look round. As far as I can remember, there were some beautiful residences overlooking the Indian Ocean, but as in all other parts of India I had seen, there were also areas of desperate poverty. In my experience, these seemed to be associated with railway stations, which provided massive shelters for the poor and destitute. I remember occasionally going into Calcutta and Bombay in the evening when we would have to pick our way through hundreds of men, women and children who were settling down for a night's sleep. If you were on a train and stopped at a station you would be moved by the clamouring of dozens of beggars, often children, holding out begging bowls. Some of them were badly mutilated, for example, having no legs below the knee. We were told that this was done to them deliberately to gain sympathy. These were the sights and sounds of India which have remained with me for the rest of my life. Since the war, I have spoken to Indian businessmen who say that the situation has not changed. We met some American crews in Calcutta whose job was to fly supplies from India to China, which had been under attack by the Japanese since 1933. In their opinion, the poverty and starvation in China was much worse, although this was hard to believe.

After three day's journey from Madras we arrived in Calcutta. We changed stations to get the train to Dhubulia. At this time we noticed a significant change in the weather. Instead of the clear skies of southern India there were huge dark thunder clouds and downpours of torrential rain, the like of which I had never seen before. This heralded the arrival of the Monsoon, which was shortly to test our flying skills to the full.

The territory in this part of India is part of the Ganges Delta. This river rises in the Himalayas and flows across northern India, eventually entering the sea in the Bay of Bengal through an enormous delta made up of hundreds of small rivers. The land is very fertile and supports a large population; after the partition of India it became Bangladesh. But there are also dangers in this very low-lying area from floods and tidal waves which have caused havoc over the years with much loss of life. However, the land was ideal for heavy bomber bases, and Dhubulia was one of several.

In three years since joining the RAF in 1942 I had been on about 15 different bases and 50 years later it is difficult to remember them all in detail, however, I do recall that we lived in concrete huts which each accommodated about 30 aircrew. It was so hot it was like living in a furnace. We kept all the windows and doors open to try to get some fresh air in the place but with little success.

The beds were called 'charpoys' and had wooden frames with a rope base. To lie on the bed, you rolled out a bed-roll which resembled a thin canvas sheet, you hung a mosquito net over the bed, smeared yourself with anti-mosquito cream and climbed into bed with a hope that you might sleep! Unless we were on flying duties we had the afternoons off, from twelve to four o'clock – the hottest part of the day. This we usually spent lying on our charpoys reading or playing cards. Luckily, my charpoy was near to one of the doors. Soon after I had laid down, a small frog would enter and sit beside the bed absolutely still. It was fascinating to watch how passing flies etc. would be snatched out of the air with a flick of the frog's tongue, as if by magic. We were also intrigued by the large flying beetles which would crash into the wall, fall to the floor, then stagger up again to try to find the open air.

There was always at least one game of cards being played by day and by night (usually poker) by chaps who could not sleep because of the heat. I often joined in a game of poker but my temperament was so cautious that I never made or lost much money, but I saw other men lose a month's pay in an afternoon and have to borrow for the rest of the month. The other popular game amongst the real gamblers was 'rolling the dice' which I never really understood.

I clearly remember one very hot, humid night, when a card game was in full swing and the atmosphere was thick with cigarette smoke. Thousands upon thousands of white grub-like creatures with wings flew through the window, attracted by the electric light. Apart from the sheer inconvenience of these creatures we were worried that they would get into our clothes and bedding. Somebody came up with the bright idea of lighting a newspaper and holding it up to the light. The smell of burning insects was unpleasant to put it mildly, but thankfully it did the trick!

One of the bright spots in all this was the presence of the *Charwalla* (tea boy) who would serve us hot sweet tea all day. We must have drunk gallons of the stuff, but it was the best way to keep cool. He had a nice little business going and we enjoyed talking to him. When we left Dhubulia he came to the runway to wave us goodbye as we took off.

We were at Dhubulia for about eight weeks and during this time we managed to get a few days leave. We spent several days in Calcutta where we found one or two nice restaurants to eat, but generally the poverty was so depressing that we were glad to get back to our base. Occasionally, George Brooker the Wireless Operator, and myself used to take the local train to Krishnagar which was half an hour's journey away. The Catholic Church had established a mission there – a fine large house in a pleasant part of the town. We would go there for an afternoon, read newspapers and books and enjoy a cup of tea and cakes.

It was always a fascinating experience to travel on an Indian train, especially so, when we sat with the local population; they always made room for us to sit down, and although most of them could not speak English and we certainly could not speak Bengali we achieved some understanding. We shared the carriage not only with the people but with their livestock as well. As the train moved off the roof of the carriage and the running boards at the sides were occupied with people jumping on at the last minute obviously to avoid payment. It was a very dangerous way to travel but they were used to it.

On one occasion we were returning back to base, and had just got on the train when we heard loud shouting from the direction of the town. We looked out of the window and saw a chap of about 20 running towards the train followed by about 50 others. The train was just moving as he jumped on, breathing a sight of relief, no doubt. But the engine driver had been alerted by all the noise and pulled the train up about a quarter of a mile from the station. The leaders of the crowd jumped on board and dragged the unfortunate chap off. Our fellow passengers said he was most likely a thief who would be giving a thorough beating.

Our other leisure activities were the usual camp cinema (described earlier) and a visit to the bar in the Mess. The drinks were plentiful and cheap, and one night a month they were completely free. The following morning the base was full of men trying to get over their evening of heavy drinking. These nights, of course were only permitted when there was no operational flying the next day!

When we first arrived at Dhubulia we were allowed the usual two days to settle down, before we were ordered to go to the main briefing room to meet the Wing Commander and his Chief Officers. We turned up at the briefing room about ten minutes before the appointed time so that we could have a look round. There was a huge map of the South East Asia war zone, which showed the enormous distances involved.

From the bomber bases in North India the map covered Malaysia and Singapore, as well as Burma and Thailand (then called Siam). You could see that there had to be hours of flying before reaching any Japanese targets. There were also pictures of Japanese fighter aircraft with details about their performance. The picture I found unforgettable was one of a Japanese officer with a Samurai sword above his head, about to behead a blindfolded British Airman. Knowing the genuine possibility of this happening to any one of us, we all felt very disturbed, but as there is so much propaganda in war, we dismissed it as all lies. Unfortunately, when the war ended it was discovered that the Japanese really did treat their prisoners with unbelievable cruelty. Thousands died through starvation and forced labour, particularly on the notorious Burma railway. Captured aircrew refusing to give information, other than number, rank and name were often executed. We learned later about the Japanese attitude to war – *bushido*. Soldiers should never surrender and to do so was shameful, whereas by dying in battle they were assured of eternal life. A very different attitude to Europeans, who were prepared to surrender and be taken prisoner if forced to.

The Wing Commander in charge of 99 Sqn was a slightly built, quietly spoken man, quite different to the Commander of 622 Squadron. He told us that the Liberator Squadrons in North India were being used to mount long-distance bombing raids on Japanese communications: railway lines, bridges, trains, shipping etc. He noted that we had all finished a 'tour' with Bomber Command but warned that our experience would be of limited value. Anti-aircraft and fighter opposition would be far less than we had experienced in Europe, and frequently we would find ourselves bombing a target on our own not with a large number of other aircraft. Coping with the long distances, the monsoon weather and the inhospitable territory would demand all our skills.

After a short spell for questions he wished us 'good luck' and then we were dismissed.

We went to the stores to collect equipment to help us in event of crash landing in hostile territory. I can remember clearly three of these items:

1. A dangerous-looking jungle knife or *machete*.

2. A handkerchief-sized piece of cloth containing a message in about fifteen local languages promising a reward to anyone

who helped an airman who had been shot down. This was commonly known as a 'goolie chit'.

3. A revolver with just six rounds of ammunition. As I recall, no instructions were ever given as to the use of the revolver. I can only imagine that in the event of coming down in the jungle, five rounds of ammunition would be used to defend oneself and the sixth to commit suicide! I cannot remember having any firing practice. Revolvers are notoriously difficult to fire accurately, so nobody had much faith in them.

Our flying from Dhubulia started with practice bombing and the usual flight round the area to familiarise ourselves with the landscape. We landed from this flight and taxied the aircraft to dispersal. Waiting to inspect the aircraft was a group of ground crew. They wore bush hats, no shirts, a pair of shorts, and socks and shoes. The sun had turned them into a chocolate colour so that they looked like native Indians. I saw one of these men staring intently at us; his face seemed vaguely familiar. After a few minutes he walked over to me.

"Aren't you Les Parsons from Ludlow?" he asked.

"Yes," I replied in astonishment. "But who are you?"

"I am Syd Faulkner," he said, "I live five doors away from your Grandmother in Ludlow!"

I had last seen him six years earlier and although we were acquaintances rather than friends, we enjoyed many a long chat about Ludlow and its people. Our relatives back home were thrilled to know we had met. Syd was an engine fitter; we were together on 99 Squadron for the next six months.

On the 22nd May 1945 at 0655 hours we took off for our first Far East Operation. Because there is a lot of work to do

ANNAMITE

Cùng anh em Việt-Nam yêu dấu,

Tôi là một quân sĩ của đồng-Minh. Tôi tới đây không có mục-đích gì để phá hại dân chúng Annam là bạn thân của tôi. Tôi chỉ muốn phá hại quân Nhật và đuổi chúng nó ra Khỏi Đông—Dương cho đặng mau chóng. Nếu các anh có thể dẫn đường cho tôi đi tới gần nới trại binh của Đồng-Minh; thì Chánh-Phủ của tôi sẽ ban thưởng cho các anh một cách rất xứng đáng.

HAKA

Ka Koi,

Kema ne Mirang ralkap ka shi. Mahin nangma ...fak pek awk ka ra lo. Ka hoi-kom nang shi. ...apan ral tuk awk ka ra. Japan mi nang khwa ram ...zok-zok htawl ka du.

Zangfak on, nangma Mirang le Amerikan ralkap ...um nak lam nai tyik a nang ka kalpi a chun, ka ...so-za ne laksawng a tam pi pek lai.

KACHIN

...hau Du ni,

Ngai gaw Ingalit hypenma rai nga ai. Anhte ...w nanhte hpe aru ara jaw na matu sa n rai. ...awan Japanni hpe Myenmung kaw na shachynt ...u na matu sa ni ai.

Khauni anhte Khau hpyenmani dap de gadum ai ...n kaw na shangun dat yang. gumhpraw sungui ...yani law law jaw na ra ai.

LAIZO

Rual,

...cimah in Mirang ralkap kasi. Rualpi... ...zai peek dingah ka ra lo. Rualpi... ...an ral hi zonzai peek ih, nan k...

MALAY

Pemberi tahu,

Sahaya soldadu kerajaan bersakutu. Datang ini, tidak sahaya mahu mengachau sahabat sahaya, anak Melayu. Bangsa yang di—lawan sahaya bangsa Jepun, sampai di-halau dari tanah Melayu dengan sa-berapa segera. Jikalau tolong sahaya, kerajaan sahaya hendak membalas budi tuan dengan chukup ia-itu bila orang Jepun itu habis di-halau.

SUMATRA

Kepada toean jang terima.

Saja soldadoe Inggeris. Datang sini, tidak saja maoe menjoesahkan sahabat saja, orang Sumatra. Dengan orang Djepoen sadja saja berperang sehingga di-oesir dari negeri Melajoe ini. Kalau tolong saja, kerajaan saja tentu membalas boedi toean dengan tjoekoep ia-itoe bila orang Djepoen itu habis di-halau.

TAMIL

The document, printed on cloth, carried by RAF Airmen in the Far East, promising a reward for their safe conduct in numerous languages. It was hoped that this would save them if they were shot down over enemy territory.

before take off we were called to get up at 0330 hours. We got dressed into flying equipment and then went to the canteen to have an early breakfast. After this, I went along to the Navigational Briefing Room to be given details of the operation to be carried out.

In 1942, when the Japanese overran large parts of South East Asia including Burma they had great problems in supplying their overseas armies because of the nature of the country with its jungles. They decided to supply their armies in Burma from Siam (Thailand). To do this, they built a railway through the jungle from Bangkok to Rangoon using prisoners of war.

During the war we were not generally aware of the terrible suffering caused by the building of this railway. As the railway emerged from the jungle it ran along the sea coast south of the Burmese town of Moulmein, it then went across southern Burma to Rangoon. This railway was vital to the Japanese and it was therefore of great assistance to the British 14th Army who were driving the Japanese out of Burma that the Liberators of the RAF should cut this important link.

It was no surprise, therefore, to be told that our mission was to attack a stretch of railway south of Moulmein with delayed action high explosive bombs. Any train we saw on this railway was to be bombed and we were to do this at very low altitude (about 200 ft). At the briefing I was given details of the route to be taken, time to be at the target, speed to fly at, weather forecast and wind etc. From this information I was able to construct a flight plan and draft a map of the area over which we were to fly.

Having completed all the necessary calculations I joined the other members of our crew at the general briefing. By this time it was about 0615 hours and we were taken out to the aircraft by lorry, climbed on board, carried out a series of tests on the aircraft and at 0655 hours we took off.

It was just getting light as we headed south over the Delta of the great River Ganges. I had the impression that there were dozens and dozens of small rivers entering the sea. The land was extremely low-lying and there were plenty of fishing boats around. We headed out over the Bay of Bengal. I can remember the sky everywhere was full of dark low clouds, with a cloud base of about 2,500 feet. You could sometimes see violent thunder storms where the clouds and rain came down to sea level. We took great care to keep away from these and flew in clear air just below the clouds.

After four hours flying over this most depressing water we hit land at the south-west tip of Burma. We then headed across more sea for another hour to the target at Moulmein. As we approached the coast there was a yell of excitement when we saw an engine with three coaches heading northwards. The driver of the train must have realised he was about to be attacked because he stopped in a deep cutting to get the maximum protection.

It was a most exciting moment as we swung into the bombing run, bomb doors open. Down the bombs went in a cluster around the train. Judging by the steam and smoke coming out of the locomotive it seemed likely that we had made at least one direct hit, but because of the delayed action fuses we did not see the actual bombs explode. We turned round and swept back along the seashore with all guns blazing in an attempt to destroy the carriages. Although the action had only lasted a few minutes, I told the skipper that our instructions were to head back out to sea before any Japanese fighters appeared.

"OK, he said, we will just do one more run and then go home". Once again the gunners started to open fire. Suddenly, I was horrified to see a man of about thirty with dark Burmese-looking skin, dressed in a pair of baggy brown trousers race from behind a sand dune and throw himself down into the railway cutting. He was probably just a local man walking along the beach and he must have been absolutely terrified by the enormous aircraft flying at 200 feet at about 200 miles per hour. From the Navigator's position in the nose of the aircraft I had a grandstand view of what was going on. After 55 years I still carry the man's image in my mind and have always prayed that he was unharmed.

The total trip there and back was about eleven hours and we said we thought the trip was satisfactory. However, the Debriefing Officer told us that the Japanese were very skilful at repairing bomb damage and that he expected them to have the railway line operational soon.

It was no surprise therefore, to find ourselves on another trip to Moulmein five days later. Our instructions were to disrupt the railway line should it have been repaired. On this occasion we did not find any trains but we blew up more stretches of the line. This happened again on the following day, so in one week we caused considerable destruction to the Japanese supply lines.

On one of these trips (I cannot remember which one) we were flying at our usual height just below the clouds when Frank Ramsey our Rear Gunner reported another Liberator about a quarter of a mile behind us flying very low over the water, saying, "I don't like the look of this, he is much too low..." Suddenly, he shouted that the Liberator had plunged into the sea and had sunk very quickly. There was nothing we could do. There was no hope of mounting a rescue as we were about half way across the Bay of Bengal. We were badly shaken and took it as a lesson not to fly too close to the water, realising that a sudden downcurrent of air could quickly force an aircraft into the sea. Movements of air in the tropics could be extremely violent, especially during the Monsoon.

Some idea of the pressure maintained on the Japanese can be gauged from the fact that following the three attacks on Moulmein we were ordered to bomb shipping near the port of Satahib. This port was important because it helped to supply the city of Bangkok. It was a 14-hour trip, half of which was in darkness. We flew the same route to Moulmein and then a further two hours over to the Gulf of Siam. Past Moulmein, the monsoon clouds broke up and we had a beautiful sunlit view of jungle-clad hills and the sea below. Satahib was clearly visible and we could see the ships in the harbour. Frank Carter the Bomb Aimer took up his position.

"I'm fed up sitting down here all the time," I told him, "I've been here for seven hours. I am going up onto the flight deck with the pilots while you do the bombing."

I crawled back through the small passageway and stood up on the flight deck. It was possible to see the harbour clearly. There was moderate anti-aircraft fire but nothing like the flak we had experienced in Germany. We were flying at about 15,000 feet as we started our bombing run. "Bomb doors open," said the Bomb Aimer, and up came the roller bomb doors. I turned round, stepped to the edge of the bomb bay and looked down. The sea was clearly visible through the open bomb bay and as we approached the shipping, down went the bombs.

It was a most peculiar feeling, observing the sea from this height, but since then I have realised that I must have been mad to stand there, because if the aircraft had been thrown around by gunfire or air currents I could have easily gone out with the bombs! Thank goodness this did not happen. Frank Carter claimed that he had hit a ship in the harbour and this was confirmed later by Intelligence reports.

By the end of May 1945 the Japanese army, which in 1944 had reached the border of India, had been driven back into Southern Burma. The British 14th Army was in fact near to Rangoon, the Burmese capital. It was clear that the next operation was to drive the Japanese from Malaysia and Singapore. It was no surprise, therefore, to be told that our next job was to disrupt railway communications between Bangkok and Singapore.

We were given the target of bombing the railway bridge at Sindhasani, a small village on the east side of Malaysia, a 16-hour return flight, the longest we had done so far. I have already mentioned that the monsoon season, with its heavy

99 SQUADRON.

Date	Hour	Aircraft Type and No.	Pilot	Duty
16 MAY	10.45	LIBERATOR B	F/O BAXTER	NAVIGATOR
20 MAY	19·30	LIBERATOR V	W/O SPEARS	NAVIGATOR
22 MAY	0655	LIBERATOR B	F/O BAXTER	NAVIGATOR
27 MAY	0603	LIBERATOR R	F/O BAXTER	NAVIGATOR
29 MAY	0240	LIBERATOR P	F/O BAXTER	NAVIGATOR
30 MAY	1055	LIBERATOR H	F/O BAXTER	NAVIGATOR

My log Book, showing several operations to attack Moulmein in Burma.

REMARKS (including results of bombing, gunnery, exercises, etc.)	Day	Night
Time carried forward :—	2935·0	154·50
Bombing	2·00	
X Country		3·35
B. ATTACKED TRAIN ON MOULMEIN Ry	12·20	
OPERATION TO MOULMEIN	11·20	
OPERATION TO MOULMEIN	7·55	2·55
OPERATION TO SATAHIB	8·05	6·05

SUMMARY FOR MAY 1945

Total Day.	41·40
Total Night	12·35
Total	54·15

Sgd   O.C. A Flt.

SUMMARY FOR MAY

OPS. HRS.	48.40
NON. OPS. HRS.	5.35
TOTAL SORTIES	4
TOTAL OPS. HRS	48.40

O.C. 'A' FLT.

TOTAL TIME ....

cloud and tremendous rain had already begun and this got steadily worse. As monsoon clouds can rise to 30,000 feet, there was no way that a piston-engined aircraft could climb 'above the weather' as is possible with modern jet-powered aircraft. We had to fly underneath the clouds or through the middle of them.

We took off on 5th June for Malaysia during a heavy storm. As we headed out over the Bay of Bengal the clouds and rain were at about sea level and it was much too dangerous to fly underneath them. We had already seen how a low flying Liberator could be sucked into the water, so we decided to fly at about 15,000 feet through the weather. The rain cascaded down in sheets and we could see nothing above, below, or ahead. After flying for some four hours in these conditions I calculated we must be somewhere near the southern Burmese coast.

Suddenly, without the slightest warning, the Liberator plunged downwards into a tremendous dive. About thirty seconds later it was flung upwards at a similar speed. It was then spun round in a tight circle, and equally suddenly was flung out of the cloud. We emerged into bright sunshine and below us, by some miracle, we could see the coasts of Burma and Malaysia.

I realised that we must have unwittingly flown into a cumulo-nimbus cloud due to the zero-visibility conditions. These clouds have very powerful up and down currents which are easily capable of breaking the wings off an aeroplane. They can rise to 30,000 feet or more, with a huge 'anvil' on top. In a hot summer in England these thunder clouds – as they are often called – are often visible. Whenever I see one, my mind flashes back to this incident over Burma.

I do not suppose that the whole incident lasted more that 45 seconds but we were all badly shaken and thoroughly frightened. During the previous two years of flying we had faced all manner of hazards, but nothing equals the sheer force of nature. We flew on for about ten minutes to get away from the storm, realising how lucky we had been to survive.

Each one of us went over his own part of the aircraft to check for damage. The bombs were still in position, the compasses were working and the engines seemed OK, so we decided to carry on to the target which was some three hours away. With the improved weather we were able to fly at a lower level and we had no problem finding the railway bridge which was successfully attacked with delayed-action bombs.

It was about 1330 hours when we started our eight-hour return flight. Near the equator it gets dark at 1800 hours, so much of the homeward trip would be in darkness over the sea and we knew that there would be more storms to face. After two hours flying over the Malaysian jungle I could see the skipper and co-pilot having a discussion, looking anxious. Rather than talk over the intercom I decided to crawl to the flight deck to find out what was going on.

"You chaps look worried. Have we got a problem?" I enquired.

"We've got problems with the oil pressure on No. 2 port engine," the skipper replied, "and we're concerned that it could catch fire. I'm afraid we are going to have to switch it off and feather it."

The consequence of this would be that the aircraft could barely climb and would also lose speed. The prospect of a safe return to India looked remote. I crawled back to my navigational position and did some calculations which confirmed how difficult it was going to be.

While I was doing this I remembered reading in the Indian papers several days earlier that the 14th British Army had advanced to a position near the airfield of Mingladon near Rangoon. This was the only airfield in the area which might be big enough to take a four-engined bomber. I said to the skipper that we should head for Rangoon, about three hours away and make an emergency landing, hoping of course that the airfield had indeed been captured by the British.

He agreed immediately and I gave him the necessary courses to get us there.

We struggled along at about 2,000 feet to the west coast which we crossed at Tavoy Island and then turned north heading for Rangoon. The rest of the trip was a constant nightmare of continuous rainstorms and low cloud, with islands suddenly appearing through the clouds. We were all praying that the other three engines would keep going; any more trouble and we would be in the drink! I kept looking for signs that we were heading in the right direction, when below us, I noticed that the sea had started to turn brown. This was a great comfort because the brown colour was mud carried out to sea by the great Burmese river, the Irrawaddy. After another hour of flying we reached the coast of Burma and I had no problem in map reading to the Mingladon airfield which was north of Rangoon.

It was nearly dusk and as we approached we could see fighters with RAF markings round the perimeter of the airfield, so thankfully we knew it was in British hands. We circled the airfield, contacted the Control Tower, explained who we were, and asked for permission to land. "Not likely!" came the reply. "We have only been here a couple of days, the main runway is still full of bomb craters, the short runway has only been filled in to take Spitfires and Dakotas and then there is a drop of thirty feet at the end of the runway." The officer of flying control said, "You will never get that thing down in one piece."

"Hard luck," said our skipper, "We've got to get down somehow."

The fact that I am able to tell you this story shows what a good pilot he was and that he did manage to bring the aircraft down successfully. We touched down just at the beginning of the runway, and after one hundred yards the skipper slammed on the brakes. The Liberator shuddered and rocked and came to rest about ten yards from the opposite end of the runway. There was a cheer and a sigh of relief from everyone. We learned afterwards that the RAF men on the ground had been placing bets on whether we would not get down alive.

After we had landed we were told to remain on the runway until the Flying Control Officer had found a place for us to park the Liberator. There were no lights on the airfield and eventually a jeep came out to us and led us to a space on the grass by the Flying Control Tower. As we climbed out of the aircraft we gave it an affectionate bang with our fists because we realised there was no way it would fly again. It was interesting to remember that the identification letter painted on the outside of the aircraft was 'K'. All aircraft had an identification letter, and in addition, a British Aircraft usually had a bomb painted on its nose for every completed operation.

The Liberators we flew in were old American aircraft and as well as bombs they painted huge pictures of famous people, mainly film stars of the 1930s. A popular film at the time was *King Kong,* the story of a huge gorilla that created havoc and terror in New York. It was no surprise, therefore, to find the Liberator 'K' had a replica of King Kong painted on its nose. For many months after the war I met airmen who had been to Mingladon and reported that the 'King Kong Liberator' was still there, gradually rotting.

After the aircraft had been parked we reported to the Flying Control Officer and messages were sent to our base in India that we were alive and unharmed.

As you can imagine, accommodation was pretty chaotic, as the Japanese had been driven out only a couple of days before. However, we managed to get hold of a quantity of straw and we bedded down on a concrete floor in a hut and, in spite of the many 'creepy crawlies' we managed to get a good night's rest. The next day we talked to some of the fighter pilots based there, and they told us a very strange story that retreating Japanese troops were discarding their uniform and dressing themselves as Burmese natives (their appearances were very similar). They were selling eggs and local produce, but hidden in their baskets were revolvers which they used on unsuspecting airmen with devastating effect. We thought that they might be joking, but to be on the safe side we remained well within the airfield boundaries.

Supplying advancing troops and so on in this sort of country with its poor roads and monsoon rains is a major difficulty, and to overcome this, many of the supplies were brought by air by the twin-engined Dakotas of the American Army Airforce. At this time, supplies were being flown from India and Northern Burma to Rangoon. After two days in Rangoon we managed to get a lift back to India in a Dakota with a returning American transport pilot and then completed our journey back to our base by rail.

In spite of this long journey and the hours we had flown there was to be no respite for us. Two days later we were given another Liberator and were sent to bomb and machine gun retreating Japanese troops in southern Burma.

A week later the Captains and Navigators of ten crews were called to a special meeting with the Wing Commander. He told us that we were being withdrawn from operations forthwith and that we would be given special training for operations which at this stage were highly secret. When I first heard this, my heart leapt with joy at the thought of no more flying over the Bay of Bengal and the Burmese jungles, but I soon became apprehensive on contemplating the vast area of South East Asia still occupied by the Japanese. It looked as if the war might last for years and I was sure that there were plenty of rotten jobs still lined up for us...

We did about two and a half weeks of intensive special training. This consisted of long low-level flights (at about

1,000 feet) over different routes in Northern India. Whilst flying around these routes we had to find targets about the size of a small field marked out with the letter 'H' in white stone. Having found the target we came down to one hundred and fifty feet and dropped large containers by parachute. The purpose of this training was a well-kept secret, for no one had any idea what it was all about. In these circumstances, rumours flourished, and a favourite one was that we were going to be dropping of spies in French Indo China (Vietnam). What a daunting prospect that would be!

By this time the war in Europe had been won in May 1945 and plans were being made to send reinforcements to fight the Japanese. I think it was in July 1945 that the results of the General Election at home were published. We were very pleased that the Labour Party had won with a big majority. Apart from many differences in home policy between Labour and Conservative, the Labour party said that they were going to give British Empire Countries e.g. India, Malaysia, Singapore etc. their freedom at the end of the war, while the Conservatives wanted to retain the British Empire as it was prior to the war. It seemed clear to me, that had the Conservatives won, we would have soon been fighting the local inhabitants to retain British control, whereas with Labour in power, we felt that we should be going home after the Japanese were defeated.

CHAPTER IX

Paradise Island

About the middle of July 1945 all the crews involved in the special training were summoned to a special meeting. We were told that we should be leaving Dhubulia for a secret destination, and that we should immediately pack our kit. To support the aircraft and crews, ground staff and their equipment would be flying with us. We were informed that we were to take the kitchen staff and their cooking equipment with us. We were given only 24 hours to complete the loading. On the 16th July the pilots and navigators reported for briefing and were given the directions to fly to an RAF base called Kankesanturai at the very northern tip of Ceylon, about a seven hour flight.

I remember it was a very pleasant flight and compared to our recent activities it was very enjoyable. None of the ground crew had flown before, so the good weather was particularly good news for them. We landed at KKS at 1400 hours. We were told to go and get tidied up and have some food and report to the Briefing Room at 1700 hours. This we did, and on entering the briefing room there was the usual huge map of the Indian Ocean and all the surrounding countries. Our destination was indicated by a woollen line which ran from KKS right down the middle of the Indian Ocean towards Australia. The line came to a halt in what looked like open sea, but looking closely we could see a small group of islands called the Cocos or Keeling Islands where an air strip had been built by army engineers a few months earlier.

I and the other Navigators collected navigational maps of the area and flight logs and drew up a flight plan. I joined up the KKS airfield in Ceylon to the Cocos Islands and literally gasped when I realised that the distance was 2,000 miles over the ocean and that it would take us approximately 13 hours to get there. The first and only land to be sighted would be the Cocos Islands. We immediately realised that any serious mechanical trouble with the aircraft would mean the end of us – there was no way we could be rescued if we came down in the sea. The weather forecast was quite good, except that we were told that there was a band of thunderstorms lying across the equator. We were instructed to fly low underneath them. Take off time was give as 1900 hours.

As we walked from the briefing room, Mac Baxter and I agreed that we would give anything to get off this trip, but we knew that we daren't disobey orders. We made our way to the aircraft at dispersal. The rest of the crew were lying on the grass near the aircraft and about 20 yards away were the Cook House staff, talking amongst themselves and looking rather anxious.

"Where the hell are we going?" asked Frank Ramsey.

"We've been told to keep it secret," I said, "but even if I told you, you'd be none the wiser. All I can say is that it won't be less than 13 hours flying time."

It was about this time that a spokesman for the Cook House staff came over to me.

"We are all getting worked up," he said. "None of us have flown before this morning and we are wondering what is going to happen at the next stage."

"We will be taking off in an hour's time at 1900 hrs and we have a 13-hour night flight," I told him.

He looked incredulous. "Bloody hell! Do you think we are going to make it?" he asked

"One thing is absolutely certain," I said, "I want my breakfast on dry land in the morning as much as you do, so I'll be working flat out all night to ensure we're on course to our destination." I must admit that as I spoke these words to quell his anxiety I was far from confident. At that time there were no modern navigational aids like satellite navigation. There was a radio signal coming from the Cocos Islands to help guide us, but experience had shown me over the past two years that such signals were not always reliable. I would have to take readings from the sun, moon and stars to check our position – never an easy job!

1900 hrs arrived and we all climbed on board. Off down the runway we went, straight out to sea, flying at 5,000 feet. After several hours flying we approached the Equator and, sure enough, there was the lightning and thunder, a pretty but menacing sight as it lit up the sea. We had to come down to 1,000 feet to pass underneath the storm clouds. After about three quarters of an hour we emerged out of them into clear skies. We flew steadily on and at about 0700 hours witnessed the most beautiful sunrise over the glorious blue-green waters of the Indian Ocean. The sky was clear except for a few 'cotton wool' clouds scattered around.

By this time I had told the rest of the crew and passengers where we heading.

"If we miss this island, our next stop will be Australia... If we have enough fuel," I said jokingly.

I remember looking at my watch and noting that it was 0800 hours. I said to everyone over the intercom, "Keep a good look-out, we should be there at any minute."

Suddenly, Frank Ramsey yelled out, "There it is! About half a mile away on the port side!"

A cheer came up from us all. Over 50 years later I still think it is the most marvellous sight I have ever seen. The coral islands with their white sand and rock, covered with coconut palms, stood out against the colourful blue sea. White waves were breaking on the coral reef surrounding the island about half a mile from the shore. You must remember that in 1945 very few people had ever flown in an aircraft, and of these only a handful had seen a coral island from the air.

The anxiety I had been feeling in the previous quarter of an hour suddenly disappeared. We gave our details to the Cocos Control Tower and were told to land. The approach to the runway was rather strange because the end of it was literally at the water's edge. As we neared touchdown the feeling was that we would land in the sea; fortunately this was an illusion. As we rolled along the runway, the wheels made a funny 'tinny' sound because the temporary runway was constructed with metal strips rather than concrete.

We taxied to the dispersal point, raised the bomb doors and jumped out to be met by a lovely warm sea breeze. Having unloaded our kit we were taken to our accommodation in the aircrew section, which consisted of tents (four to a tent) 250 yards from the runway and 50 yards from the shore. We found that the island was already home to many army and navy personnel to protect the islanders against possible Japanese invasion.

If you look at a map of the Indian Ocean you will see that the Cocos Islands lie at a latitude 12 degrees south of the Equator and a longitude of 96 degrees east. They are a small cluster of coral islands, covering only a few square miles, shaped like a horseshoe, with the open end near the Equator.

Their history was not easy to discover, but we understood that they were first developed in the 19th century by a Scottish trader called Clunies Ross. He brought in a few

Aerial view of the Cocos Islands airstrip.

people from Malaysia and they settled on Home Island; a small island but the most suitable for growing crops. Administration was eventually taken over by the British Government. In 1976 they were handed over to Australia.

Apart from the people on Home Island the islands were uninhabited until the military command in South East Asia decided to build an airbase on the southwest island, the only one big enough for a runway to take four-engined heavy aircraft. It was rumoured that this part of the island was uninhabited because it was only a few feet above sea level and occasionally had been swamped by tropical storms.

Although, a long way from being the most isolated place in the world, nevertheless it felt very lonely to us. I have already explained that we had to cross 2,000 miles of ocean to get there. The nearest land was Sumatra, 800 miles away, which at this time was still occupied by the Japanese.

Our first concern when we arrived was how to tell our families in the UK where we were. All we could quote was a Field PO number and as all mail was heavily censored, there was no real way of informing them. Nowadays, if servicemen are involved in overseas wars there are instant radio and television links so their families at home have knowledge of their whereabouts. Good communication with loved ones is important for the morale of men and women stationed thousands of miles from home. Every effort was made to provide a fast airmail service, but even so, in the Cocos Islands it could take up to three weeks to hear from home.

The climate on the Cocos Islands was ideal. The hot temperatures near the Equator were modified by a constant sea breeze of 10-20 mph, so the average temperature was about 75 degrees, and in the months we were there, we experienced only light showers of rain. What a relief after the humidity and heavy storms we endured in Northern India!

When we had unloaded our kit into our tent, our first job was to walk to the seashore and to have a look at the beautiful blue/green sea. It looked ideal for a swim, but a notice had been left in each tent, warning about the danger of being cut on the sharp coral. In fact, I seem to remember that to report sick with injuries from the coral, was a punishable offence.

About 25 yards from the shore, near to our camp was a coral reef about four feet high and about forty yards long, it provided some protection against the open sea. When the tide was out, the water was about eight inches deep and it was quite safe to paddle. You could see the most beautiful small fish in the sea. However, when the tide started to come in there was a transformation. The water quickly rose to five or six feet, and the current was so strong that it was difficult to stand upright even a few feet from the shore. It was possible to be swept away unless you were extremely careful. Swimming was impossible.

When you go on holiday in England, particularly to Cornwall, you will see notices warning people of the dangers of the sea, but in spite of this, there is always someone who ignores the warnings and gets drowned, often taking would-be rescuers with them. This situation was also true in the Cocos Islands; the warnings were ignored. From time to time aircraft flew to Ceylon to pick up urgent supplies, and on one occasion it was our turn to do this trip. When we returned we found an air of gloom hanging over our friends. The story came out as follows. About a quarter of a mile further along the coast was a camp of RAF ground crew. Two of them had managed to get hold of a rubber dingy. They put it in the water and got in to it but it soon started to drift with the current and they realised they were getting into difficulty. The alarm was raised and the medical officer was notified, he being a very strong swimmer. He decided that the only hope of rescue was by forming a human chain. Several of our friends volunteered, and eventually reached the dingy.

However, the strength of the current was too great, and the chain broke. Five rescuers and the two men in the dingy were swept out to sea. Apart from human remains found on the shore, the men were never seen again. Their bodies would have been eaten by sharks and barracudas. This incident remains uppermost in my mind whenever contemplating swimming in the sea – which I have not done since!

Returning to our first day on the islands, while we were on the shore, we remembered that as we had walked from the airfield to the tent, we had passed through groups of palm trees with windfall coconuts lying on the gound. Until then, the only coconuts I had ever seen were on 'coconut shies' at the Ludlow 'May Fair'. You paid tuppence for six wooden balls and any coconut you knocked off the stand, you could keep. It wasn't until I got to the Cocos Islands that I realised that on the palm the coconut is encased in a green husk, which has to be cut away to reveal the hard kernel inside.

We could not resist the temptation of free coconuts, so we went back to our tent, collected our jungle knives and made our way back to the coconuts. They were absolutely delicious, but we were soon to discover that it was possible to have too much of a good thing. On day one I ate three coconuts; day two, two coconuts and on day three I drank the coconut milk. I have never eaten coconut since!

Reading the previous paragraphs about the Cocos Islands you could be forgiven for thinking that the RAF had sent us to a tropical island for a holiday. But we knew this was not so and that it would not be long before we were fully engaged in fighting the Japanese. There was no official word yet as to what our role was going to be, but there were plenty of rumours. The other members of the crew were frequently asking me what was going to happen, and I used to say, of course that I did not know, except by looking at the maps of the area. We were about 800-1,000 miles from Singapore and Malaysia. This was much nearer than our bases in northern India had been, and I said that I thought we were bound to be involved in some way with the liberation of these territories. All we knew was that it would be a week or so before the squadron was organised to fly on operations, especially as there was a big maintenance job to be done on all the aircraft.

We therefore enjoyed the respite as best we could. After we had been on the island about two days we were sitting in our tent, talking, when there was a rustling outside. The flap of the tent was pulled back and two dark-skinned islanders entered and sat down. They must have been about thirty years old and spoke good English. They were most friendly and told us they lived on Home Island, just across the lagoon with their wives and families, and spent much of their time fishing and making ornaments out of coconut shells, they also grew their own crops. As I recall, the total population was about 600 and we understood the rule was that if any of them left to live elsewhere (e.g. Malaysia) they were not allowed to return, presumably because of the risk of spreading discontent among the islanders about their way of life.

After we had talked for a while they produced a round dried milk tin, took off the lid and passed it round. Inside were pieces of grass on which nestled some delightful cakes their wives had cooked and sent to us as a gesture of greeting and friendship. We had learned in the Far East to be careful about eating native food, but these cakes were delicious and melted in your mouth. In exchange we gave them whatever gifts we could find, mostly cigarettes.

Surprisingly, one of our main topics of conversation was football! The English club Arsenal was then known worldwide and they were keen to know all about the team.

They warned us of the dangers of the open sea and said, that if we liked, they would take us for a sail on a much safer lagoon. During the few months we were there, we did this several times and it was marvellous to see all the beautiful coloured fish in the clear blue waters.

Another warning they gave us was to keep clear of the land crabs that lurked all over the island in crevices beneath coconut trees. They were the size of a man's hand and very well camouflaged. The first thing one would see was two eyes on stalks looking at you; a nip from their large claws could be most painful.

With the stationing of so many troops on the island there was a lot of waste food about. Often the supply ship which called from Ceylon once a month was found to have rotting food on board which had to be thrown away. This must have been a major cause of the rapidly growing rat population on the island. At night, they used to scamper across the top of the tent – not very pleasant. The food we ate was mainly tinned. (It was here that I ate dehydrated potatoes for the first time. They were like wet tea leaves; horrible, to put it mildly!)

Our main consolation was that we had plenty of cheap Australian drink. Apart from drinking we had an open-air cinema which sometimes could be exciting when the screen blew over in the middle of a film and had to be re-erected!

Although the airfield and the area around was strictly out of bounds to the islanders, they were free to wander round the accommodation area and on most days we could see them doing a spot of trading. However, they were strictly forbidden to bring over their wives, children or girlfriends (except on the day Japanese surrendered, when the ladies brought over an extra supply of cakes in celebration). Home Island where they lived was equally out of bounds to service personnel unless it was an organised trip. I seem to remember one such trip to see a football match and I recall how clean and smart their huts were.

We had been on the island only a few days when another astonishing coincidence occurred. If you look at the map you will see that the Cocos Islands are on the direct route from Ceylon to Perth in Australia which in those days could be an 18-hour flight. After the airfield had been opened and a squadron of Spitfires stationed there for its protection, it was decided to use the Cocos Islands as a refuelling stop between Ceylon and Australia. Therefore, as well as RAF Transport, aircraft from KLM and QANTAS Airlines made use of this facility. To pass the time away we would go down to the airfield and watch these aircraft take off and land.

RAF Transport flew the large, American, four-engined Skymaster. We were sitting by the control tower one day when we saw one of these aircraft land. It taxied to a halt near to where we were sitting. The crew jumped out followed by the captain. He was a stocky man, about five feet six tall, with a slight wobble as he walked.

"I know that chap!" I said to my friend, and as they walked close to us I called to him "Do you remember me? Les Parsons from Ludlow?"

He turned around and recognised me immediately. The captain of the aircraft was Arnold Jones, who I had last seen in 1937 when he was a 'messenger boy' at our local ironmongers! He had a very distinctive walk, hence his nickname – 'Wobbler'. He told me that when he left the ironmongers he volunteered for the RAF. He qualified as a pilot and flew transport aircraft from Karachi in India to Sydney Australia, calling at Bombay, Colombo, Cocos and Perth. We both thought it was quite amazing to have met each other in such a remote place, especially so, when I told him, another Ludlovian was there. He spent a night every now and then on the Cocos Islands during his transport flying. This story has a very sad ending, however. A few months later we heard from his colleagues that he had contracted polio in Bombay and had died soon afterwards.

After we had been on the island about a week the aircrews were summoned to a meeting at which we were told that operational flying would be resumed shortly. We were given a few general comments on the military situation, but we were not given full details, presumably in case we were shot down and tortured by the Japanese to obtain information. Usually meetings were conducted by senior RAF Officers but in this case we noted that there were senior Army Officers present as well.

You will remember that the war in Europe began in 1939. In the Far East the Japanese had begun the invasion of China in the early 1930s and this war was still going on in the 1940s. In December 1941 the Japanese navy attacked the American naval base at Pearl Harbour in Hawaii and at the same time, the Japanese army invaded British, American, French and Dutch territories in the Far East. By February 1942, most of these had been captured.

By late 1941, the British Government became aware of the Japanese threat and sent thousands of troops to reinforce Malaysia and Singapore. Unfortunately, many of these troops arrived in Singapore to find it already held by the Japanese.

They were marched straight from their troop ships into prisoner of war camps. It was possibly the greatest defeat ever suffered by the British Army. The Japanese found their surrender incomprehensible as their philosophy was to fight to the death. This goes some way to explain their cruel attitude to prisoners of war.

However, many prisoners escaped from labour camps and formed guerrilla bands in the Malaysian hills from where they mounted attacks on the Japanese supply lines. Many Chinese and Malays joined these bands and when plans were made to liberate Malaysia and Singapore from the Japanese, these bands were to play an important role in attacking the Japanese. For them to do this successfully, meant supplying them with plenty of modern equipment and ammunition.

It was to be the job of the RAF Liberator Squadrons on the Cocos Islands to drop these supplies, and for this purpose, we came under the control of the British Army. The intensive training we had been given in northern India, low flying and dropping containers by parachute, suddenly fitted into place.

Within a few days we had begun air testing the aircraft and flying around the Cocos Islands to familiarise ourselves with local flying conditions. In early August 1945 we began operational flying and were summoned for our first briefing. As we thought, the main directions were given by a senior Army Officer.

Apparently, these guerrilla bands were in camps in the highlands near Kuala Lumpur and had set up secret dropping zones with individual code names in the hills. They were in contact by radio with headquarters in Ceylon and would arrange a time and place for supplies to be dropped. This information was in turn transmitted by headquarters to the Cocos Islands. It was then up to the RAF Liberators to drop the supplies.

As far as I can remember only one aircraft at a time was sent to a dropping zone. Our first drop was to a DZ called TIDEWAY 1180 SD. I have no record of its latitude or longitude but I do remember that it was in the hills.

Our directions were to fly at low levels to reduce the chances of being spotted by the Japanese. We had to arrive over the dropping zone at 4 pm, about two hours before darkness, so that the guerrillas could collect the supplies and make off further into the hills before the Japanese could surround and capture them. Our only means of identifying the DZ, which was just a clearing in the jungle, would be the letter 'H' made in white stone and the smoke from a small fire. We were told that the part of Sumatra over which we whould be flying was very isolated and unknown to Europeans. We should, therefore, make sure we had with us our revolvers, ammunition and jungle knives in case we came down. We carried a full crew of air-gunners and were told that we were 'on our own' with no fighter escort.

I had calculated that the return flight would take us about twelve hours, so by taking off at 10 am we should be over the DZ by 4 pm and back at base by 10 pm. It was a beautiful day when we set off for Sumatra. From some way out at sea we could see the range of mountains which ran along the West Coast at a height of about 10,000 feet. When we were a good way from the coast we had to climb steadily, keeping as low as possible over the mountains. We then passed over the plains of Sumatra, which looked very inhospitable, with swampy ground and many streams and rivers. We flew over the land at about 1,000 feet, but to reach Malaysia we had to cross the straits of Malacca – 50 miles or so across.

As we approached the sea we came down to 150 feet. I have already mentioned how exhilarating low flying is, but of course it is also highly dangerous and a small mistake can lead to fatal consequences as there is little room to manoeuvre. We flew over many small boats which looked like Chinese fishing junks and from my position in the nose I could see the startled look on the faces of the fisherman as our huge plane passed over them. The DZ was in the hills beyond Kuala Lumpur. These hills rose to around 3,000 feet, so having crossed the coast we started to climb. By this time it was 3.30 pm and I calculated that we should reach the DZ at 3.50 pm. We flew in amongst the highlands, expecting to see the arranged smoke signal, but there was nothing except hills and jungle. When you have flown six hours over strange territory only to find that you cannot find your target, it produces a nasty feeling in the pit of the stomach. If we could not find the DZ we faced three main dangers:

Firstly, the longer we flew around, the more likely it became that the Japanese would spot us and send up fighters to attack us. Despite of the fact that we were heavily armed, I would not have rated our chances very highly if it came to an air battle with a squadron of Zeros.

Secondly, there was the danger of flying into high ground when we were concentrating on looking for the DZ.

Finally, we could not afford to hang around too long. We had a six hour return trip to the Cocos, with the underlying worry that we might run out of fuel on the way back.

We decided that we could spend about half an hour searching the area. I remember thinking that the map I was using was none too accurate because I could not find some of the landmarks it indicated.

I remembered my training and said to myself "This is like trying to find a small field on Snowdon in North Wales."

We were about to give up our search but I am pleased to report that his was one of those occasions when fortune smiled upon us. We flew down one valley and drew a blank, turned into the next one and there, about three miles away, I saw a wisp of thin smoke. We flew closer and identified the white 'H' in the corner of a small clearing. We could see the guerrillas in the trees. Our training in dropping containers from low-level now paid off, and apart from the odd container which hit the trees, the majority landed safely in the clearing. We circled round, watching the men collecting the containers. We came low enough to wave each other 'goodbye', hopefully giving them enough time to return to their camp in the hills before dark.

We settled down for our return flight, but our problems were not yet over... As we crossed the Malacca Straits we could see clearly the 10,000 ft mountain range over which we had to fly. But this was the Equatorial Region in August and the tremendous heat of the day had caused the build-up of huge banks of Cumulo-Nimbus clouds along the whole length of the mountain range.

After our near-fatal encounter with one of these clouds in Burma, we knew that we would have to fly over the top of them to be safe. It looked as if we would have to fly at about 25,000 feet to remain in clear air. We had something of a dilemma because we were still low flying to prevent discovery by the Japanese and we did not want to start climbing too early. Fortunately, having dropped the containers, the aircraft was relatively light, so we postponed our decision to climb for as long as possible. Despite many moments of anxiety, we succeeded in clearing the storms with a few hundred feet to spare and looked down on the storm clouds with relief.

We landed at Cocos safely at 10 pm and made our way to enjoy a 'flying meal'. Needless to say, none of us were exactly thrilled at our new role in the war.

(As a matter of interest, at the de-briefing we were told that a radio message had already been received from the guerrillas to the effect that most of the packages from our 'drop' had been successfully picked up.)

At about 11 pm we retired to bed with a few bottles of Canadian Lion beer, which was very strong and very quickly put us in a relaxed frame of mind. We all agreed that it would not be long before invasion forces landed in Malaysia, and once this had happened we could see our role changing from dropping supplies to bombing and gunning Japanese troops.

Someone suggested that what was needed was "something to blow Japan up." We all laughed at this, because it was just wishful thinking. Little did we realise, how near to the truth it proved to be...

In spite of our tiring day flying and going to bed late, we were up as usual at 7 am and went to the mess tent for breakfast at 7.45. I cannot remember the menu, but I am sure it involved dried egg! In the mess tent we had radio speakers which broadcast the news in English from 'All India Radio' in Delhi. The news started at 8 am, and today there was a dramatic announcement saying that a few hours earlier, US Super Fortresses based in the Pacific Islands had dropped an 'atomic bomb' on Hiroshima, Japan. This revolutionary weapon had the explosive power of 20,000 tons of TNT and the city had been almost destroyed. The US government called on Japanese forces everywhere to surrender.

When we heard this news, however, we laughed in disbelief. The Americans, in peace and in war, had a reputation for exaggeration, and we thought this to be another of their boastful claims. At school I had studied some elementary chemistry, which I did not really understand, but do remember being told that if you 'split the atom' there would be a gigantic chain reaction and the whole world would fall to pieces! Evidently this could not be true, if this was indeed an atomic bomb! During the rest of the day we listened avidly to every news bulletin. They confirmed the dreadful devastation and loss of life. Aside from sympathy for the victims, our main hope was that the Japanese would now surrender and we would be relieved of our dangerous duties. Unfortunately, there was no sign of it, so the war went on...

On the day following the dropping of the Atomic Bomb, Mac Baxter and I were summoned to the Flight Commander's office. We were told that on the following day we were to accompany a crew who had not flown on any operations before. We were to leave our own crew behind and were to act as the 'Screen Navigator and Pilot'. Our job was to keep overall watch on the flight, giving the new crew the benefit of our experience. At the same time, we were not to interfere in the details of the flight. This called for some tact, especially as the pilot of the new crew was a Flight Lieutenant and senior in rank to all of us. Fortunately, they were very nice chaps. The night before the operation, we all met and had a few beers and Mac Baxter and I were able to answer some of their queries.

We had to report for briefing at 7 am on the following morning and we were told that it was to be a longer trip than our previous one. Once again the main briefing was carried out by Army Officers and we were told that the dropping zone was to be FUNNEL 509 SD. I cannot remember the latitude and longitude but I do remember that it was further into the Malaysian hills than our first trip.

The crew navigator did all the initial calculations and he asked me to check them for him. We agreed that it would be about a 15 hour flight. We decided that I could be the most help by getting another map of the area and helping with the map reading, because in low level flying it is easy to get lost.

Mac Baxter and I were wished good luck by the rest of our crew who now returned to the sea-shore, lucky devils! In the meantime at 8.50 am we clambered aboard and took off for Malaysia, the bomb bays once again filled with containers.

The route to Malaysia was almost the same as the one we had taken three days earlier. We found our experience was invaluable. Once more we realised that our greatest chance of avoiding discovery by the Japanese was through low flying. I remember that we flew even lower than on our first flight and after about seven hours we reached the jungle and mountainous area to the east of Kuala Lumpur. This was where the dropping zones were located.

We again had difficulty in locating the actual drop zone. What a nightmare it was flying up and down these mountain valleys! Fortunately, after about thirty minutes I saw the tell-tale blue wisp of smoke that told us we had arrived. The procedure for dropping the containers was repeated. I was not in the navigator's position in the nose of the aircraft, so I sat on the floor near the edge of the bomb bay and when these were opened I had a clear view of the ground 150 feet below. I could see the men in the trees very clearly.

We made a 'good drop' onto the zone and I watched as the guerrillas ran out to collect the containers. We made a final circle before waving goodbye to each other. I wondered at the time whether they were better off on the ground than we who had the prospect of a seven-hour flight back to Cocos Islands, but on reflection I concluded that our position was preferable. After all, they had been under Japanese occupation for three and a half years.

You will remember that on our first flight over Sumatra we had been horrified to find a bank of Cumulo-Nimbus clouds over the western mountains. Mac Baxter and I had hoped that this was an isolated incident and that when we returned this time these clouds would not be there. No such luck! As we crossed the Straits of Malacca, heading across Sumatra (it was getting dusk around 5.30 pm) we could see a huge barrier of thunder clouds. We judged their height to be about 25,000 feet. The pilot said he doubted whether the aircraft could get up that high, but there were only two alternatives: either fly through them or over the top. The crew members had no experience of flying through such clouds and therefore were mostly unconcerned, but Mac and I were scared stiff and Mac continually urged the pilot to go higher and higher. In the end, the Liberator reached 28,000 feet, the highest we had ever flown, but as we approached the cloud it still towered 1,500 feet above us. The pilots decided that we should all put on our parachutes and stand by the escape hatches, because there was no way in which we were going to get over the top of the clouds. So, with a slightly 'nose down' attitude to pick up speed, we headed 'straight through'.

Even at the top of the clouds the air currents were strong enough to throw the aircraft about, but after about ten minutes of being buffeted we emerged into clear air on the other side with a 'relief cheer' from everyone. We could see the Indian Ocean far below us but we had still got four hours of flying to reach our destination. We arrived at about 11pm and asked for permission to land. We were told to go ahead, and so we started the 'landing drill'.

Suddenly, we heard some violent swearing from the pilots on the flight deck. The nose wheel had become jammed, and in spite of every effort to release it, it remained jammed, so we had the prospect of having to land on the two main wheels. While the pilots remained on the flight deck, the rest of us took up our crash positions in the back of the aircraft.

Once more we prayed for our survival. The pilots brought the aircraft down safely, but of course, as it slowed the nose dipped and ran along the metal runway, sending showers of sparks everywhere, with the possibility of fire and explosion. When the aircraft finally came to a halt we leapt out of it, even though there was a drop of ten feet or so to the ground. We raced away and the ground fire fighting crew managed to stop any fire from spreading.

After such an incident-filled operation it took quite a time for us to be debriefed after landing and it was consequently about 1 am before Mac Baxter and I got back to our accommodation tent. Here we found the rest of the crew waiting up for us, with a few bottles of beer already opened. They told us that they could hear us circling round the island and that the news of our troubled landing soon had spread around. This was a real emergency for the rescue services. Fortunately, everything turned out alright.

I have no idea how many aircraft in total were lost in operations from the Cocos Islands, I do recall three Liberators lost: one blew up on take-off, one landed in the sea off Sumatra and the third crashed somewhere in the jungle. With the huge distances involved and the inaccessibility of the terrain, there was no hope of mounting a rescue. This thought horrified me at the time and whenever I have thought of flying in the years since I cannot get the jungle, the sea, and the tropical storms out of my mind.

Just imagine, therefore, my feelings when we were told to prepare for yet another operation in two days time.

It was now five days since the dropping of the first atomic bomb and there was no sign of the Japanese surrendering. Two days later, on 15th August 1945 the Americans announced that a second atomic bomb had been dropped on the city of Nagasaki with the same devastating results. Once again, the Japanese were called on to surrender immediately. This time, the Emperor of Japan (who was regarded as a god by the Japanese) assumed control, overruling his military leaders. He ordered the immediate cessation of hostilities.

Much to our relief, flying from Cocos Islands was cancelled until British Headquarters had moved from Ceylon to Singapore, where they would formally accept the Japanese surrender.

Immediately the war was over, pressure built up for men to be demobilised and returned to civilian life. However, there was a huge job involved in disarming the Japanese and freeing all the prisoners of war who were in camps situated in the jungle.

To help solve these problems we began flying once more – to Malaysia and Sumatra only this time, and the containers were full of food and medical supplies for POW camps. These operations were just as hazardous with regard to the natural obstacles, but at least there was no longer any threat from the Japanese...

During September 1945 we took off for four flights to the camps, but at this time the servicing of our aircraft had deteriorated – mainly because of the lack of spare parts – and we had to return on two of these occasions because of engine failures that brought us close to ditching into the ocean. On the other two occasions we successfully reached the POW camps, and it really was a great thrill to see hundreds of prisoners outside their huts waving and cheering. Looking back over the years I feel the dropping of supplies to these camps was one of the most worthwhile and satisfying jobs we ever did.

About seven weeks after the war had ended we were flying on another POW mission and had got roughly three hours out to sea and were nearing Sumatra when again, one engine failed and we lost power on a second, causing the aircraft to rapidly plunge from 5,000 feet down to 2,500 feet before we were able to level out. We had no alternative but to return to the Cocos Islands. I suddenly felt myself shaking all over, and however much I tried I could not stop it. When we got back to the Cocos Islands there was a church service being held on the seashore alongside the runway. As we touched down, the unbalanced power due to the loss of one engine caused the aircraft to swing across the runway towards the church parade. It rapidly scattered and we ended up on the sea-shore after swinging off the runway!

Liberators of 99 Squadron on Cocos runway.

CHAPTER X

My Flying Career Ends

The shaking I had experienced in flight would not stop when I got onto the ground and I thought that I had contracted a tropical disease like Malaria. I had to report sick to the MO but he could find no infection. He quickly diagnosed that I had nervous fatigue due to so much flying over the past two years. I was flown to see a specialist in Ceylon who confirmed the diagnosis and ordered that I should have six months rest from flying. By this time it was three months after the end of the war and flying had already been drastically reduced. Air Crews were being disbanded and many members were being sent home for demobilisation. The government had devised an ingenious formula for calculating when everyone could be released from the forces. This took into account a man's age and length of service and, therefore, everybody had a 'release number'. The government would then announce release numbers and the release dates. My own number was 46 and it was therefore possible to calculate that I would be released in about September 1946; 11 months ahead.

After I had been grounded, I was posted with about ten other aircrew to RAF Headquarters in Colombo, Ceylon. My service record was examined and it was found that before joining the RAF I had been studying accountancy, so they found me a clerical job with one or two other men in the Air

Priorities Board. At this time there was a great demand by important business people, service personnel, MPs etc. for flights to the UK. Passenger seating availability was very limited because there were few passenger aircraft, so we had the job of sorting out who should go first, and issuing the necessary tickets. There were ten of us in the office, headed by a Squadron leader. The staff included two Sinhalese people, who we got on extremely well with. We were accommodated in buildings that were normally government offices, near to the seafront. Because of the heat, we worked from 7 am until 1 am. It was all very pleasant. I thought Colombo was the most pleasant city I had seen in the Far East. There did not seem so much poverty. It was possible to catch a local bus and go about five miles south to a beautiful surfing beach near the Mount Lavinia Hotel. Nearby was a Buddhist Temple, which we were shown around. We also saw lace-making in progress.

The RAF Headquarters had its own football team and although I was not very good at it I managed to enjoy a few games. It was an extremely pleasant place and only a few hundred yards to the seafront from which it was possible to see beautiful sunsets as the sun went down over the India Ocean. With no likelihood of flying again I slowly began to feel much better.

Being stationed in the centre of Colombo I was within walking distance of the shops cafes and cinemas. I found a very nice cafe that I was able to visit on most afternoons and, although I cannot remember the detailed menu, the two things I can remember were the delicious lemon tea and fresh local pineapples. This has been my favourite fruit ever since, and I think of Colombo whenever eating it. One afternoon in December 1945, I was having my usual afternoon tea when three airmen walked into the cafe and came and sat down at the table. They were very thin and their skin looked yellowish. When we got talking, they told me they had been prisoners of war in Sumatra since 1942 and were now on their way home. They had been badly undernourished and they told me that some prisoners had been ill-treated by the guards. Their first real knowledge that the war had ended came when low flying Liberators dropped food and medical supplies in 'clearings' near the camp. However, their exhilaration was dampened when one of the Liberators crashed killing all aircrew. I told them that I had been a Navigator with 99 Squadron and that this had been our main job after the war ended. Talking to these chaps confirmed that we had been doing a very worthwhile job.

My work in the Air Priorities Board was mostly routine, but I think it was in January 1946, I turned up at the office as usual to find a crowd of agitated people waving their air tickets, and asking what was going on, as there were no flights leaving Colombo. This was news to us, but later we were able to piece the story together. As I have already explained, once the war had ended, the one thought in people's minds was to get back to the UK and to civilian life. In order to apply pressure to get this done, the ground crews at the large air bases of Karachi, Bombay, Colombo and Singapore had gone on strike, thus bringing to a halt all air communications. This was a serious situation, for the operation of any armed service relies on absolute obedience to orders given by superior officers. This disobedience on a small scale could be dealt with by a court martial, but a strike of so many men made this impossible for senior RAF officers to deal with. This problem was really a political matter for the government in London. Fortunately, at this time there were several members of Parliament touring the Far East. One of them was a Labour MP named Harold Davis, who was a close friend of Prime Minister Clement Attlee. A large hall was commandeered for a meeting in Colombo which everyone on the Base had to attend. Harold Davis listened to the complaint and made what was probably one his best political speeches, promising to take these grievances to the Prime Minister in London. I think these meetings saved the situation because within a few days air traffic was flying normally. Eventually, I remember, three people were arrested in Singapore and Court Martialled as the ring leaders.

One afternoon in February 1946 I was playing football for a local RAF team. The ground was hard and bumpy and, rather clumsily, instead of kicking the ball I kicked the ground. A terrible pain shot up the back of my right leg and if I had had any sense I would have left the field right away. Instead I played on. Overnight it became most painful and as I hobbled into the office the following day I was greeted with some sympathy. At 9.30am a telephone rang and my friend Gerry, who answered the call, said "It's for you."

The call came from the orderly room, and the clerk on the phone said, "Are you W/O Parsons?"

I replied in the affirmative.

The voice said, "We are sending you to the UK on a month's leave. You have two hours to get packed and report to Colombo Harbour Gate."

"Someone is pulling my leg!" I said

"Not at all," the voice replied, "it is perfectly true. Come to the office and collect the necessary papers."

The thought of going home for a month gave me a wonderful boost, and in spite of limping badly, I arrived on time. I sent an airmail to Eileen saying I expected to be home sometime in March. I said goodbye to all my friends and told them I would be back in May.

I could not carry all my flying kit so I left some of it behind and struggled along to the orderly room to collect the necessary leave passes. It appeared that these leave arrangements had been made at very short notice. The French troop ship *Pasteur* had been to Saigon which was then the capital of French Indo-China. It had taken on board French prisoners of war who were being repatriated to France through the French Port of Toulon, after which, the ship was going to Southampton. The ship called at Colombo for refuelling and RAF Headquarters were told that a party of about a hundred RAF men could be taken to the UK. I have never understood why I was selected as one of these, but I accepted the chance with gratitude.

I managed to join the party at the dock gates. I knew no one but I quickly made friends with three Londoners. I was expecting the troop ship to be docked against the quayside, instead of which it was anchored in the middle of the harbour. It was a ship of about 27,000 tons and we were told it was too big to dock against the quay. To board it we had to climb down into a motor boat, which would take us across the harbour, to climb up steps on the side of the ship, and enter through the side of it. When I saw what had to be done I said to the three chaps from London, "I will never manage to get on board with my injured leg".

"Nonsense!" They said. "We'll get you on board, even if we have to carry you!" – Which was virtually what they did.

By the time we got on board we were all exhausted. Charlie, one of the chaps, said, "Before I joined the RAF I was a masseur with Chelsea Football Club and I'll give you some treatment for your leg once we have settled down." He was as good as his word and gave me three lots of treatment – agony, to put it mildly – but it cured the problem.

We left Colombo and sailed across the Arabian Sea, and on into the Red Sea. The heat was terrific, well over 100 degrees. The *Pasteur* had been a French luxury liner before the war, travelling from Southampton and Cherbourg to New York, but like most other liners it had travelled the world as a troop ship for six years. Consequently, we found the conditions most unpleasant. We slept on straw mattresses which were alive with all manner of insects. After a few days at sea we all began to have skin irritations which kept us awake at night. We did not see much of the French prisoners but those we did see looked quite ill. After about eight days we reached the southern end of the Suez Canal where we dropped anchor to await our turn to go along the canal and into the Mediterranean. Here again I later learned of a coincidence involving someone from my home town Ludlow.

Before the war, I had a friend named Ken Grant, who had a small photographic business. After joining the army he was sent to India. On the day we anchored at Suez, several troop ships arrived from India, and Ken was on one of them. True to his profession he would take pictures of anything of interest, and later on I found out that he had taken one of the *Pasteur*. I was delighted when he presented me with a splendid picture of the ship.

Although we were only at anchor for 24 hours, it seemed endless and a great cheer went up when the Pilot finally came on board. Slowly but surely we passed along the Canal and made our way into the Mediterranean. After the tremendous heat of the Red Sea it came as a shock to discover how cold it was in the Med. We soon swapped our tropical kit for winter RAF uniform. By this time (February 1946) the war had been over for many months, so ships were able to proceed at full speed and by a direct route.

The *Pasteur* headed for Toulon. It was interesting when passing through the Straits of Messina between Italy and Sicily, to see the island of Stromboli, which was then, and probably still is, an active volcano, which every few minutes puffed out volcanic smoke and ash. We then passed between Corsica and Sardinia and headed for Toulon, which had for many centuries been France's most important Naval base. Most of Napoleon's adventures had started from there. At the outbreak of war in 1939, France had a very powerful fleet based at Toulon. Britain and her allies were most concerned that this fleet should not fall into German hands after the defeat of France in 1940. The German Army made a dash for

Toulon to try to capture the fleet, but French Naval Commanders prevented this by sailing into Toulon's outer harbour and scuttling the ships. Although I had heard reports of this, it was weird as we approached Toulon to see the once proud French Navy lying on the bottom.

As you can imagine, there were crowds waiting to greet the French prisoners of war and we could see from the ship many scenes of reunion between the relatives which were extremely moving. It took some time for the Frenchmen to disembark and to leave the dockside, when this finally happened, we were told that we could have six hours ashore, before the ship sailed for Southampton. I was still friendly with the Londoners I had met in Colombo and so we made our way into the town. Everything there looked very drab, it seemed to consist of narrow cobbled streets and most of the shops in the centre were still affected by wartime shortages. However, we did manage to buy some French perfume for presents to take home. After a while, we saw a wine bar and we went in for a drink, it was crowded and a couple of Frenchmen recognised the RAF uniform, and shouted out *"Ere is ze brave boys of ze RAF!"* An enormous cheer went up and they began to buy us drinks. To this day, I cannot remember how we found our way back to the ship, but I suspect some kind Frenchmen helped us. There is no doubt they were genuinely pleased to see us.

It was about 10pm when we started to throw off the effects of the party at Toulon and we could feel the motion of the ship as it slowly sailed into the Mediterranean on its way to Gibraltar and then on to Southampton. As it sailed into the sea, the ship started to roll from side to side. We were told that there was a strong gale force wind blowing from the Spanish coast and hitting the *Pasteur* broadside. I knew nothing about ships but when I joined the *Pasteur* at Colombo I noticed that it was very high out of the water. Rumours said, that when it sailed across the Atlantic in very rough weather there was a danger of it capsizing and that the ship's captain was terrified! This was obviously a rumour, but even so, the 24 hours sailing from Toulon to Gibraltar was terrifying and we all were afraid the ship was about to capsize. It was also the only time at sea that I have felt really seasick, so when we saw Gibraltar in the distance we all cheered in relief.

By contrast, the Atlantic was quite calm and in a few days we sailed past the Isle of Wight and into Southampton Water. What a wonderful feeling it was to see English shores again, even though they looked very wintry and covered with snow. As we headed up towards Southampton docks we passed a liner carrying British girls who had married American servicemen in England, who were going to join their husbands in America, and were known as 'GI brides'.

We were all glad to get off the *Pasteur* after four weeks sailing. Afterwards we were put on a train to the RAF personnel depot at West Kirby, near Liverpool.

You will remember that after a few days on the *Pasteur* I got some skin irritation on my legs. Unfortunately, there was no treatment available on the ship so it became very uncomfortable. I had no alternative than to report to the MO at West Kirby. Just imagine my frustration having travelled 6,000 miles for a month's leave only to end up in a RAF hospital! On examination, the MO found that I had an infestation of black insects under the skin – Scabies. No wonder I had been feeling unwell. I do not know what the present treatment is, but in those days it consisted of having a hot bath, scrubbing the skin with a wire brush until it was broken, followed by applying a purple ointment to kill the insects – a most painful and unpleasant experience. Fortunately, this treatment soon got to work and after a week I was able to go on leave for the remaining three weeks, after which I again reported to West Kirby to begin my return journey to Ceylon.

When I was on leave there was an official announcement in the papers saying that RAF members with release number 46, which was my number, would be demobilised in the middle of August. My return journey to Ceylon would take about six weeks and this meant that within a few weeks of my return I would have to start again to come back to the UK in order to be demobbed on time. Therefore, when I returned to West Kirby I confidently expected to be told that I would be kept doing odd jobs in England for the last few months of my service. Unfortunately, nothing was further from reality!

I was called into the Wing Commander's Office and told that he had notification that I could be promoted to Commissioned Officer if I was prepared to sign up for another two years flying service. If I did this I would not be returned to the Far East. I was given half-an-hour to think it over. I quickly decided not to take this offer but to go for demob in August. Although the war was over, there were still many conflicts going on in the world and as I had already had so many near escapes whilst flying that I did not want to tempt fate again.

So it was that in late April 1946 I found myself once more in the Liverpool Dockyard waiting to embark. This time I would be travelling on another pre-war liner – the SS *Britannic* – whose destination was Bombay. The contrast between the journey in January 1945 could not have been greater. For instance, there were no more than 800 of us, which meant there was plenty of room. I had a comfortable cabin to myself. The food was good, and the spring weather was beautiful. Radio programmes were broadcast throughout the ship and these included a live commentary on the first FA Cup Final since 1939. I think it was between Derby County and Burnley and Derby County won. The ship travelled the usual route via Gibraltar and the Med and it was sheer luxury.

As we approached Port Said at the northern end of the Suez Canal rumours circulated around the ship that people due for release up to September 1946, of which there were many on the boat, would all be landed at Port Said. These rumours turned out to be true, and about the middle of May I found myself ashore at Port Said together with many others, including several other Air Crew. Apparently the intention was to send us to a Transit Camp outside Cairo to await transport back to the UK. (What a money waster!)

We quickly sensed that the relationship between the British and the Egyptians was far from good. In 1942 Egypt had been under threat of invasion by the Germans who were defeated by the British under Montgomery at El Alamein. Far from being grateful to the British, the Egyptians wanted us out of there. Although it was interesting to see places like Cairo and Port Said, one had to be extremely vigilant. There were many instances of service personnel being killed by terrorists throwing bombs outside service camps. I felt the whole atmosphere was full of tension, although we did manage to find a nice swimming club in Cairo.

Three of us ex-Aircrew used to go around together and one afternoon we were having a drink in a famous wine bar called Groppi. A very smartly dressed and obviously wealthy Egyptian came over to us and said, "I am very sorry for the poor relationship between Britain and Egypt and I would like to make it up to you. If you will meet me on the Nile Bridge on Sunday at 1 pm I will show you all the sights and historical interests and take you out to dinner afterwards."

We agreed to do this, but on reflection decided that the risk of kidnapping and murder was too great, so we did not turn up. I have often wondered about it, but all things considered, I think we did the right thing.

After two months hanging around in Egypt, where thieving was so widespread, we had the splendid news that in two days time we were to be returned to the UK. Several hundred of us were taken by lorry to a railway terminal on the shores of the Suez Canal called Casfareet. The idea was to board a troop train the same night to be taken to the Egyptian Port of Alexandria. The train was absolutely packed and of course very hot. At the end of each carriage was an open platform where you could stand outside to keep cool. These observation platforms were loaded with kit bags as well as the standing personnel. We had been travelling for about a couple of hours when we saw the lights of a village, suddenly the train began to slow down and we could hear shouting and an Egyptian climbed onto the observation platform and started to try throwing the kit bags off the train. We managed to push him off, but unfortunately he was just a decoy because behind us another Egyptian had succeeded in throwing off four kit bags, one of which was mine. A few miles further on the train came to a halt and the general idea was that we should march back to the village to retrieve the stolen bags. However, the train guard told us to forget it, as he feared many of us would be killed if we got involved. The last thing I wanted to do was end up dead in Egypt having survived the war, so the train resumed its journey to Alexandria. When daylight came, crowds of Egyptians threw stones at us and I thought "I shall be jolly glad to get out of this country!"

One of the big problems in getting back to the UK was the long sea route. Nevertheless an ingenious scheme had been introduced, by which troops coming from the Middle and Far East were shipped to Toulon in Southern France from where they were taken by special troop trains to Calais and then on to Dover, this saving four or five days travelling. So, having arrived at Alexandria I found myself on board the Troop Ship *Devonshire* on which I had another splendid Med cruise to Toulon. After a three-week wait at Toulon I found myself back in the UK.

It was not yet the end of July 1946 and so I spent the last three weeks of my RAF service at Uxbridge on Administrative work until the wonderful day on the 14 August 1946 when I collected my double breasted, blue, pin-striped suit and mackintosh and other clothing and stepped out onto Civvy Street... and thus ended my eventful four and a half years as an RAF Navigator.